Puzzle Pieces from God

Puzzle Pieces from God

Marie McDermott

True gratefulness, praise and thanks to God--The Father, Son and Holy Spirit that guided me through this book.

5

Puzzle Pieces from God

Marie McDermott

WHAT AM I DOING WRONG?

I am not here to list your sins or to tell you what you are doing wrong. I am here to spread the word on what God considers right, according to the bible. If you feel that after reading this book, you have changes to make, then that is between you and God. I wish you the best of luck in your life and I hope you find your way to God.

If you feel angry at things I state in this book, know that I am just relaying messages from God, as quoted in the bible, but pertaining them to current times. Look deeper. It probably isn't me you are mad at, but yourself for disobeying God's commands.

By reading what God expects of the human race, you will be able to find where you may be lacking and where you may be making your own rules that are not approved by God. Here are some eye-opening words of advice, straight from the bible.

If you feel like you are living in an endless circle of repetitive motions and are bored with the same result—and unfulfilled heart—you may need to look deeper for answers on how to fix this never-ending cycle of unhappiness. You are missing pieces, and you can only get them from God.

Life consists of many different categories. Each one will be taken and broken down and defined according to what God wants based off the bible. Quotes will be given so as to not appear "judgy." This is not judging—but spreading the word of God. Life is short and each day you wake up, you are given a new opportunity to be forgiven of the old actions and live with new intent—based off God's will. Don't wait until it's too late—change while it still matters.

⛶ Puzzle pieces that are needed to make your life complete lie within these categories and will also be listed and summarized in the In Summary portion. You can find any of the puzzle pieces you need in any aspect of your life, and not just within the categories listed below.

- BELIEF IN THE TRINITY OF GOD
- WORK
- HOME
- MARRIAGE
- PARENTING
- CHILDLESS LIFE
- SINGLE LIFE
- SEXUAL CONDUCT
- FRIENDSHIP
- CHARITY

- IMAGE
- FAITH/VIRTUE
- SOCIETY
- WHEN PEOPLE ARE MEAN
- NEEDS & WANTS
- MOVING FORWARD
- PUZZLED?

I hope this book contains the answers you were looking for. God is guiding me as I write this, and he is guiding you as you read it.

We wake up and repeat the same things each day. One day quickly turns into a week, then a month, then you blink, and another year has passed. The thought that crosses most minds during this long, tedious, repetitive rat race is, "What is the point to life?" We work so hard to make money to buy things that can't go to the grave with us. Why?

We are born and raised to work hard so we can gain "success" and "security." We are told that the more money we make, the more material items we can afford, and the more "successful" we will be. Here on Earth, money = success, power, and security. That is all that matters, right? Not even close. What if I told you that everything you were raised to believe is a lie?

Your parents didn't mean to lie to you! I'm not calling them liars! What they taught you is everything that was taught to them. "The American Dream" is the ultimate goal in America. The job, house, spouse, kids, minivan, soccer games, and apple pie. If you are living each day and coming up empty at the end of the day, even though you have attained everything the American Dream consists of, keep reading. Life is not about the American Dream. Now you know. The American Dream as we know it is a goal that leads to broken commandments and a collection of sins. In reality, the American Dream is a nightmare that gets us all off track from the real purpose and true meaning of life.

It is time to put away your pre-conceived notions about life and the meaning of life and open your mind, heart, and soul to new knowledge that I am about to share with you.

I am not an expert on life. Just like you, I have been stumbling as I go--figuring out what does and doesn't work. I have picked up the bible to find answers many times in my life. It wasn't until I opened my mind **_and_** my heart that the words came to me clearly.

Recently, I opened the bible for answers and the meanings were crystal clear. I couldn't put it down. I got it! I wanted to spend every second telling people the secret to life! I wondered to myself why I never saw the answers before! I mean, it is so clear! I am writing this book to inform people like me how to live for a purpose much larger than money—GOD.

⛶ Let me begin small. I will expand as I go. The 10 Commandments are basic laws of life given to us by God. Having a complete life **is not given by following the ten commandments, but they are the most important framework for living the Godliest life you can. The ten commandments are a puzzle piece to a big puzzle , which when put together gives you the answers you need from God to create a full life.**

All 10 commandments must be followed to get one of the puzzle pieces.

We all know God has 10 commandments he wants us to follow while we are in our Earthly bodies. The 10 Commandments of GOD are (KJV):

1. *Though shalt have no other god before Me.*
2. *Though shalt not make unto thee any graven image, or any likeness of anything that is in heaven above or that is in the Earth beneath, or that is in the water under the Earth.*
3. *Thou shall not take the name of the Lord thy GOD in vain.*
4. *Remember the sabbath day, to keep it holy.*

5. ***Honour thy father and thy mother: that thy days may be long upon the land which the LORD thy God giveth thee.***

6. ***Thou shalt not kill.***

7. ***Thou shalt not commit adultery.***

8. ***Thou shalt not steal.***

9. ***Thou shalt not bear false witness against thy neighbor.***

10. ***Though shall not covet thy neighbour's house, thou shalt not covet they neighbor's wife, nor his manservant, nor his maidservant, nor his ox, nor his ass, nor anything that is thy neighbor's.***

What do they mean? Let's break them down.

THE TEN COMMANDMENTS

COMMANDMENT 1: *Though shalt have no other god before Me.*

Don't worship other gods. There is only one God--in the form of the Father, the Son, and the Holy Spirit. God is the power behind and the creator of everything. He not only created the heavens, and Earth and everything within, but he also created a human form of himself (Jesus) to spread the miracle that God is, but in a form other human beings can understand. The Holy Spirit is the form of God in each of us. God is in every one of our hearts, if we let him in. In order to truly believe in God, you have to believe in the trinity that God is. (Father, Son, and Holy Spirit) and invite him in and believe in the love and power he brings to your life once you let him.

Jesus said, *"And I will pray the Father, and he shall give you another Comforter, that he may abide with you forever; Even the Spirit of truth; whom the world cannot receive, because it seeth him not, neither knoweth him: but ye know him; for he dwelleth with you and shall be in you."* John 14:16-17 (KJV)

***COMMANDMENT 2: Though shalt not make unto thee
any graven image, or any likeness of anything that is in
heaven above or that is in the Earth beneath, or that is in
the water under the Earth.***

God created everything on this planet. There is no need to
recreate anything into a statue/sculpted form. This kind of
connects with idolizing and worshiping different Gods.
When someone or something God ultimately created is
recreated in a non-living state, the recreation is a form of
idolizing/worshiping. Since it is a human creation and
replicate of a God-made living creation, it is a false entity.
Some may wonder if it is okay to make a statue of Jesus to
worship. Probably not. That statue is not really Jesus --it
also is a false entity, and it is not necessary to make Jesus
into a statue since you should pray to God in Jesus name
and the Holy Spirit resides inside you. Instead of praying to
statues and man-made objects, people should pray to God,
in Jesus' name.

*"Cursed be the man that maketh any graven or
molten image, an abomination unto the LORD, the work of
the hands of a craftsman, and putteth it in a secret place
and all the people shall answer and say, Amen."*
Deuteronomy 27:15 (KJV)

"Every man is brutish in his knowledge: every founder is confounded by the graven image: for his molten image is falsehood, and there is no breath in them. 15 They are vanity and the work of errors: in the time of their visitation, they shall perish." Jeremiah 10:14 (KJV)

COMMANDMENT 3: *Thou shall not take the name of the Lord thy GOD in vain.*

The word vain is defined by Merriam Webster as,

1. "too proud of your own appearance, abilities, achievements, etc."

2. "having no success: not producing a desired result."

Given that there are two ways to take the meaning of vain, here are two ways you can take the commandment. Either way, you probably shouldn't do either one.

1. "too proud of your own appearance, abilities, achievements, etc." Using God's name as your own. For instance, "I am like God--perfect in every way."

2. "having no success: not producing a desired result". Using God's name unnecessarily--as in cursing. I won't even write the two words together here. But people who throw around the word Damn after His name make those

who love God cringe and pray for those who use his name in such a dark way.

COMMANDMENT 4: *Remember the sabbath day, to keep it holy.*

Sunday is the holy day--it is the day of sabbath. *"But the seventh day is the sabbath of the LORD thy God: in it thou shall not do any work, thou, nor thy son, thy daughter, they manservant, nor thy cattle, nor thy stranger that is within thy gates."* Exodus 20:10 (KJV)
Why, you ask? Because God said so.

"Thus, the heavens and the earth were finished, and all the host of them. And on the seventh day God ended his work which he had made; and he rested on the seventh day from all his work which he had made. And God blessed the seventh day and sanctified it: because that in it he had rested from all his work which God created and made." Genesis 2:1-3 (KJV)

"Six days may work be done; but in the seventh is the sabbath of rest, holy to the LORD: whosoever doeth any work in the sabbath day, he shall surely be put to death." Exodus 31:15 (KJV)

COMMANDMENT 5: *Honour thy father and thy mother: that thy days may be long upon the land which the LORD thy God giveth thee.*

As an adult, it is normal to have your own opinions and Sometimes they have the answers you need, other times they don't. It is not acceptable to disrespect the words of the elders. Even if you don't agree, acknowledge their advice with respect and move on accordingly.

"Children, obey your parents in all things: for this is well pleasing unto the Lord." Colossians 3:20 (KJV)

"Likewise, ye younger, submit yourselves unto the elder. Yea, all of you be subject one to another, and be clothed with humility: for God resisteth the proud, and giveth grace to the humble." 1 Peter 5:6 (KJV)

"Rebuke not an elder, but intreat him as a father; and the younger men as brethren." 1 Timothy 5:1 (KJV)

COMMANDMENT 6: *Thou shalt not kill.*

Hopefully, nobody will want to attempt to break this commandment. Breaking any commandment is bad, but this is one of the deadly sins. This act is evil and will surely lead to death.

"Whoso killeth any person, the murderer shall be put to death by the mouth of witnesses: but one witness shall not testify against any person to cause him to die. Moreover ye shall take no satisfaction for the life of a murderer, which is guilty of death: but he shall be surely put to death." Numbers 35:30-31 (KJV)

"But if a man come presumptuously upon his neighbor, to slay him with guile; thou shalt take him from my altar, that he may die." Exodus 21:14 (KJV)

COMMANDMENT 7: *Thou shalt not commit adultery.*

Many people find loopholes in this commandment. It is actually a pretty clear commandment, and some people believe if they find a loophole, it lessens the severity of the action. It does not. God's law is God's law, and your feelings don't change that fact. Some people think marriage is only attained if they go to the courthouse or church and perform a ceremony that says they are married. This is true—in many states. But that is only state law, and not God's law. Before we can define adultery, we must first define marriage as God sees marriage. Jesus said,

"Have ye not read, that he which made them at the beginning made them male and female, And said, For

this cause shall a man leave father and mother, and shall cleave to his wife: and they twain shall be one flesh? Wherefore they are no more twain, but one flesh. What therefore God hath joined together let no man put assunder. " Matthew 19:4-6 (KJV)

There are many verses in the bible regarding marriage and adultery. Adultery is evil.

"It is good for a man not to touch a woman. Nevertheless, to avoid fornication, let every man have his own wife, and let every woman have her own husband. Let the husband render unto the wife due benevolence: and likewise also the wife unto the husband. The wife hath not the power of her own body, but the husband: and likewise also the husband hath not power of his own body, but the wife." 1 Corinthians 7:1-4 (KJV)

"But I say unto you, That whosoever looketh on a woman to lust after her hath committed adultery with her already in his heart." Matthew 5:28 (KJV)

"But whoso commiteth adultery with a woman lacketh understanding: he that doeth it destroyeth his own soul." **Proverbs 6:32** (KJV)

"What? know ye not that he which is joined to an harlot is one body? for two, saith he, shall be one flesh." 1 Corinthians 6:16 (KJV)

COMMANDMENT 8:   Thou shalt not steal.

Why would anyone want to steal anything? There is never a need to take something that does not belong to you. Even in a situation where you are needing food to survive, and there is no food around—God will provide if you ask and believe. In addition to asking and believing, you also have to work. God will provide hard workers with everything they need. Don't pray for a designer dress and expect it to appear. That is not how it works. You need clothes, but not a designer dress. God will supply all your needs—anything else is just glutton.

Jesus said, *"Wherefore if God so clothe the grass of the field, which to day is, and tomorrow is cast into the oven, shall he not much more clothe you, O ye of little faith? Therefore take no thought saying, What shall we eat? or What shall we drink? or, wherewithal shall we be clothed? (For after all these things do the Gentiles seek:) for your heavenly Father knoweth that ye have need of all these things. But seek ye first the kingdom of God, and his righteousness; and all these things shall be added unto you. Take therefore no thought for the morrow: for the morrow shall take thought for the things of itself. Sufficient unto the day is the evil thereof." Matthew 6: 30-34*

Work hard, pray hard, and believe hard and you won't ever have to steal.

"For even when we were with you, this we commanded you, that if any would not work, neither should he eat." 2 Thessalonians 3:10

That designer dress is not a necessity. True treasures can't be stolen, and they live in your soul. Love, the light of God, faith, honesty, trust, peace, and other true things are the only treasures worth anything real. You can't take that other stuff with you. Is stealing something worth your soul? NO.

Jesus said, *"Lay not up for yourselves treasures upon earth, where moth and rust doth corrupt, and where thieves break through and steal: But lay up for yourselves treasures in heaven, where neither moth nor rust doth corrupt, and where thieves do not break through nor steal: For where your treasure is, there will be your heart also."*

COMMANDMENT 9: *Thou shalt not bear false witness against thy neighbor.*

By neighbor, God doesn't mean just your next-door neighbor, but fellow people in the community. In this case, brother doesn't mean as in a sibling, but as a fellow man.

" Then both the men, between whom the controversy is, shall stand before the LORD, before the priests and the judges, which shall be in those days; And the judges shall make diligent inquisitions: and behold, if the witness be a false witness, and hath testified falsely against his brother; Then shall ye do unto him, as he had thought to have done unto his brother: so shalt thou put the evil away from among you. And those which remain shall hear, and fear, and shall henceforth commit no more any such evil among you. And thine eye shall not pity; but life shall for life, eye for eye, tooth for tooth, hand for hand, foot for foot. " Deuteronomy 19: 17-21

Who is your neighbor? In a parable Jesus told, when asked what a neighbor was, he defined neighbor as this:

"A certain man went down from Jerusalem to Jericho, and fell among thieves, which stripped him of his raiment, and wounded him, and

departed, leaving him half dead. And by chance there came down a certain priest that way: and when he saw him, he passed by on the other side. And likewise a Levite, when he was at the place, came and looked onto him and passed by the other side. But a certain Samaritan, as he journeys, came where he was: and when he saw him, he had compassion for him, And he went to him, and bound up his wounds, pouring oil and wine and set him on his own beast, and brought him to an inn and took care of him. And on the morrow when he departed, he took out two pence,, and gave them to the host, and said unto him, Take care of him; and whatsoever thou spendest more when I come again, I will repay thee. Which now of these three, thinkest thou, was neighbour unto him that fell among the thieves?" And he said, He that showed mercy on him. Then Jesus said unto him, *"Go and do likewise."* Luke 10 : 30-37 (KJV)

In short a neighbor is referred to not the person living next door to you, but as a person out in the community. A fellow child of God. A person who helps others. Do unto others as you want others to do unto you. Anyone who lives this way is a neighbor.   So be a neighbor to others.

"And as ye would that men should do to you, do ye also to them likewise." Luke 6:31 (KJV)

"But love ye your enemies, and do good, and lend, hoping for nothing again; and your reward shall be great, and ye shall be the children of the Highest: for he is kind unto the unthankful and to the evil." Luke 6:35 (KJV) This is a perfect description of a neighbor.

COMMANDMENT 10: *Though shall not covet thy neighbour's house, thou shalt not covet they neighbor's wife, nor his manservant, nor his maidservant, nor his ox, nor his ass, nor anything that is thy neighbor's.*

KJV bible dictionary defines covet as:

To desire inordinately; to desire that which it is unlawful to obtain or possess; in a bad sense.

See Commandment 9 to review the definition of neighbour.

Many people spend most of their lives trying to "keep up with the Joneses," only to find themselves still unhappy and exhausted. People try to match and beat the accomplishments and possessions of other people so much that they don't even realize that none of it matters in the true picture of life. You see someone with a new phone—

then you find yourself wanting the phone so much it haunts you. You see someone in a better house, and you think, "If only I had a house like that!"

You spend all your time longing for everything that everyone around you has and you don't open your eyes to the blessings that surround you in your own life. So what if you have a fancy new SUV, a fancy house in a trendy subdivision and brand-new furniture within? You keep wanting more and more and more and still feel empty with every new purchase. Why the empty feeling? Because there is a hole in your soul that can't be filled with shiny new items, beating out the neighbor in a promotion, or strutting down the road in new expensive name brand athletic shoes. There is a hole in your soul, and it can only be fulfilled by one thing—GOD.

"The prince that wanteth understanding is also a great oppressor: but he that hateth covetousness shall prolong his days." Proverbs 28:16 (KJV)

> **"Let your conversation be without covetousness; and be content with such things as ye have: for he hath said, I will never leave thee, nor forsake thee."** Hebrews 13:5 (KJV)

he said unto them, Take heed, and beware of covetousness: for a man's life consisteth not in the abundance of the things which he possesseth. " Luke 12:15 (KJV)

"Incline my heart unto thy testimonies, and not to covetousness." Psalms 119:36 (KJV)

GIFTS FROM GOD

If you invited God into your heart, you received a gift of the Holy Spirit. The Holy Spirit manifests in each of us once we invite God into our heart. We will each accept the gift of the Holy Spirit in a different way. What gift(s) do you hold? How are you using your gift(s) to please God? It is important that we use the gift(s) for good and not for evil. Using the gifts in the wrong way will result in them being taken away. Paul explained the spiritual gifts in 1 Corinthians. This will also help you understand better.

"Now concerning spiritual gifts, brethren, I would not have you ignorant. Ye know that ye were Gentiles, carried away unto these dumb idols, even as ye were led. Wherefore I give you to understand, that no man speaking by the Spirit of God calleth Jesus accursed: and that no man can say that Jesus is the Lord, but by the Holy Ghost. Now there are diversities of gifts, but the same Spirit. And there are differences of administrations, but the same Lord. And there are diversities of operations, but it is the same God which worketh all in all. But the manifestation of the Spirit is given to every man to profit withal.

For to one is given by the Spirit the word of wisdom; to another the word of knowledge by the same Spirit;

To another faith by the same Spirit; to another the gifts of healing by the same Spirit;

To another the working of miracles; to another prophecy; to another discerning of spirits; to another divers kinds of tongues; to another the interpretation of tongues:

But all these worketh that one and the selfsame Spirit, dividing to every man severally as he will.

For as the body is one, and hath many members, and all the members of that one body, being many, are one body: so also is Christ.

For by one Spirit are we all baptized into one body, whether we be Jews or Gentiles, whether we be bond or free; and have been all made to drink into one Spirit.

For the body is not one member, but many. If the foot shall say, Because I am not the hand, I am not of the body; is it therefore not of the body? And if the ear shall say, Because I am not the eye, I am not of the body; is it therefore not of the body? If the whole body were an eye, where were the hearing? If the whole were hearing, where were the smelling?

But now hath God set the members every one of them in the body, as it hath pleased him.

And if they were all one member, where were the body?

But now are they many members, yet but one body.

And the eye cannot say unto the hand, I have no need of thee: nor again the head to the feet, I have no need of you.

Nay, much more those members of the body, which seem to be more feeble, are necessary:

And those members of the body, which we think to be less honourable, upon these we bestow more abundant honour; and our uncomely parts have more abundant comeliness.

For our comely parts have no need: but God hath tempered the body together, having given more abundant honour to that part which lacked.

That there should be no schism in the body; but that the members should have the same care one for another.

And whether one member suffer, all the members suffer with it; or one member be honoured, all the members rejoice with it.

Now ye are the body of Christ, and members in particular.

And God hath set some in the church, first apostles, secondarily prophets, thirdly teachers, after that miracles, then gifts of healings, helps, governments, diversities of tongues. Are all apostles? are all prophets? are all teachers? are all workers of miracles? Have all the gifts of healing? do all speak with tongues? do all interpret?

But covet earnestly the best gifts: and yet shew I unto you a more excellent way." 1 Corinthians 12:1-31 (KJV)

⚮ Find your gift and use it to the highest capacity to please God by using it for the proper cause—to help others in whatever way you have been called. If you can't find the gift, or don't feel the gift, **it may be time to invite God into your life and accept him as your savior and open your heart to the Holy Spirit. It isn't a decision to take lightly. Once you do this, it is imperative you live for him and remove all old sins from your life.** Then and only then will you be saved, living in the spirit, and seeing your spiritual gifts in light and action. **This is one of the puzzle pieces to the true meaning of life.**

If you are not ready for this big change, don't pretend you are.

"For if we sin willfully after that we have received the knowledge of the truth, there remaineth no more sacrifice for sins, But a certain fearful looking for of judgment and fiery indignation, which shall devour the adversaries.

He that despised Moses' law died without mercy under two or three witnesses: Of how much sorer punishment, suppose ye, shall he be thought worthy, who hath trodden under foot the Son of God, and hath counted the blood of the covenant, wherewith he was sanctified, an unholy thing, and hath done despite unto the Spirit of grace?

For we know him that hath said, Vengeance belongeth unto me, I will recompense, saith the Lord. And again, The Lord shall judge his people.

It is a fearful thing to fall into the hands of the living God. But call to remembrance the former days, in which, after ye were illuminated, ye endured a great fight of afflictions; Partly, whilst ye were made a gazingstock both by reproaches and afflictions; and partly, whilst ye became companions of them that were so used.

For ye had compassion of me in my bonds, and took joyfully the spoiling of your goods, knowing in yourselves that ye have in heaven a better and an enduring substance. Cast not away therefore your confidence, which hath great recompence of reward. For ye have need of patience, that, after ye have done the will of God, ye might receive the promise.

For yet a little while, and he that shall come will come, and will not tarry. Now the just shall live by faith: but if any man draw back, my soul shall have no pleasure in him. But we are not of them who draw back unto perdition; but of them that believe to the saving of the soul." Hebrews 10:26-39 (KJV)

BELIEVE IN THE TRINITY OF GOD

No matter how much you try to be a good person, if you don't include God in your life, you will ultimately fail. God wants you to include him in all your decisions and to let him guide your life. Many times over we ignore the little voice of reason, or that bad feeling inside when we go the wrong way. This is God speaking to us. God warns us with little signs, yet we repeat our behavior and trample over all the warnings he brings--validating ourselves with excuses. Deep down we start believing we are right, but everything is falling apart. It falls apart when we don't include God in our lives and ignore his clear signals. If you ignore him, he will start to ignore you.

"For the eyes of the Lord are over the righteous, and his ears are open unto their prayers: but the face of the Lord is against them that do evil." 1 Peter 3:12 (KJV)

"But your iniquities have made a separation between you and your God, and your sins have hidden his face from you so that he does not hear." Isaiah 59:2 (KJV)

"The LORD is far from the wicked: but he heareth the prayer of the righteous." Proverbs 15:29 (KJV)

"He that turneth away his ear from hearing the law, even his prayer shall be abomination." Proverbs 28:9 (KJV)

"He that believeth on the Son hath everlasting life: and he that believeth not the Son shall not see life; but the wrath of God abideth on him." John 3:36 (KJV)

"Because I have called, and ye refused; I have stretched out my hand, and no man regarded; But ye have set at nought all my counsel, and would none of my reproof: I also will laugh at your calamity; I will mock when your fear cometh; When your fear cometh as desolation, and your destruction cometh as a whirlwind; when distress and anguish cometh upon you. then shall they call upon me, but I will not answer; they shall seek me early, but they shall not find me: For that they hated knowledge, and did not choose the fear of the LORD: They would none of my counsel: they despised all my reproof. Therefore shall they eat of the fruit of their own way, and be filled with their own devices. or the turning

away of the simple shall slay them, and the prosperity of fools shall destroy them. But whoso hearkeneth unto me shall dwell safely, and shall be quiet from fear of evil." Proverbs 1:24-33 (KJV)

God is larger than life, yet he is life. He is in everything and of everything. He created himself in Jesus to give us a better understanding of his works through an identical entity. Jesus died on the cross to cleanse us of our sins and resurrected to show us the power of God through his works. God is in each of us. This is the trinity of God. The Father (God), the Son (Jesus) and the Holy Spirit (inside your heart—if you ask him in).

Believing in the Trinity of God brings a surge of trust, faith, and power to your life. Knowing no matter where we go, God is with us, helps us realize that no matter what happens in life, God will protect us. Ask him for help, thank him daily, include him in your decisions—and listen to the answers he provides. This is a huge puzzle piece. The catch? Truly believing is necessary. Following the motions because the book said so will get you nowhere. You HAVE to feel him in your soul, and never doubt his abilities.

⊞ **Believing in the Trinity of God is a major part of the puzzle of the true meaning of life.** Life is like a puzzle in a way. We are given the correct pieces, but until we fit them all together correctly—every single one, the puzzle isn't quite right. The true meaning of life isn't one thing—it's a box of puzzle pieces to put together and show you the whole picture. When one piece is missing, it is important to search deep into your soul and pray you find it.

"Whosoever shall confess that Jesus is the Son of God, God dwelleth in him, and he in God." 1 John 4:15 (KJV)

"He that is of God heareth God's words: ye therefore hear them not, because ye are not of God." John 8:47 (KJV)

"I thank my God always on your behalf, for the grace of God which is given you by Jesus Christ." 1 Corinthians 1:4 (KJV)

"For ye are bought with a price: therefore glorify God in your body, and in your spirit, which are God's." 1 Corinthians 6:20 (KJV)

"But ye are not in the flesh, but in the Spirit, if so be that the Spirit of God dwell in you. Now if any man

have not the Spirit of Christ, he is none of his. " Romans 8:9 (KJV)

> *"If we live in the Spirit, let us also walk in the Spirit."* Galatians 5:25 (KJV)

> *"God is a Spirit: and they that worship him must worship him in spirit and in truth."* John 4:24 (KJV)

> *"Go ye therefore, and teach all nations, baptizing them in the name of the Father, and of the Son, and of the Holy Ghost"* Matthew 28:19 (KJV

In order to believe in the trinity, you have to have knowledge of God. Knowledge goes a lot deeper than just saying his name—it is learning about the miracles of life and a lot of the wonder within it. Knowledge is great, but without wisdom, it is difficult to live for God. **Wisdom is a puzzle piece to the true meaning of life.** To gain wisdom, you must absorb God into your mind, body and soul and desperately seek to learn more. Take the knowledge and combine it with truthful perspective and sound judgment, filter it through your heart and apply God's will to it to create a morally sound interpretation of the information gained. Using wisdom in all of your activities and decisions will help it grow even more.

"For there is not a just man upon earth, that doeth good, and sinneth not. Also take no heed unto all words that are spoken; lest thou hear thy servant curse thee: For oftentimes also thine own heart knoweth that thou thyself likewise hast cursed others. All this have I proved by wisdom: I said, I will be wise; but it was far from me. That which is far off, and exceeding deep, who can find it out? I applied mine heart to know, and to search, and to seek out wisdom, and the reason of things, and to know the wickedness of folly, even of foolishness and madness" Ecclesiastes 7:20-25 (KJV)

"Wisdom is the principal thing; therefore get wisdom: and with all thy getting get understanding." Proverbs 4:7 (KJV)

"For wisdom is a defence, and money is a defence: but the excellency of knowledge is, that wisdom giveth life to them that have it." Ecclesiastes 7:12 (KJV)

"O ye simple, understand wisdom: and, ye fools, be ye of an understanding heart." Proverbs 8:5 (KJV)

"Through wisdom is an house builded; and by understanding it is established." Proverbs 24:3 (KJV)

"It is as sport to a fool to do mischief: but a man of understanding hath wisdom" Proverbs 10:23 (KJV)

"Which things also we speak, not in the words which man's wisdom teacheth, but which the Holy Ghost teacheth; comparing spiritual things with spiritual." 1 Corinthians 2:13 (KJV)

"Who is as the wise man? and who knoweth the interpretation of a thing? a man's wisdom maketh his face to shine, and the boldness of his face shall be changed." Ecclesiastes 8:1 (KJV)

WORK

Work. Most people need to get a job to pay the bills. Some people cannot go to work due to health conditions.   Some people stay home to care for their kids. Work doesn't just take the form of leaving the house to go to a building and performing tasks for 8 hours before coming home. Work doesn't always have to equal a paycheck, either. There are moms that stay at home to take care of the house and kids. Stay at home moms don't get a paycheck, but they are working hard. Cooking, cleaning, taking care of children's needs, shopping, budgeting, chauffeuring—the list is endless. If you are a stay-at-home mom doing these tasks, never underestimate your importance.

Whether a person gets a paycheck or not, as long as they are performing important tasks, they are working. Sitting on the couch and eating chips while watching movies isn't work. Just to clear that up. In addition to the people who earn a paycheck and the people who work all day and don't earn a paycheck, there are people who don't work or earn a paycheck, who live off free money and do nothing for it—even when they have capability to earn money. Rest is good, but there is a time for rest and it shouldn't take the place of your daily work.

"Man goeth forth unto his work and to his labour until the evening." Psalms 104:23 (KJV)

"I must work the works of him that sent me, while it is day: the night cometh, when no man can work." John 9:4 (KJV)

"Be ye strong therefore, and let not your hands be weak: for your work shall be rewarded." 2 Chronicles 15:7 (KJV)

"Say not, I will do so to him as he hath done to me: I will render to the man according to his work." Proverbs 24:29 (KJV)

"For even when we were with you, this we commanded you, that if any would not work, neither should he eat." 2 Thessalonians 3:10 (KJV)

"Six days thou shalt work, but on the seventh day thou shalt rest: in earing time and in harvest thou shalt rest." Exodus 34:21 (KJV)

"She looketh well to the ways of her household, and <u>eateth not the bread of idleness.</u> Her children arise up, and call her blessed; her husband also, and he praiseth her. Many daughters have done virtuously,

but thou excellest them all. Favour is deceitful, and beauty is vain: but a woman that feareth the LORD, she shall be praised. <u>Give her of the fruit of her hands; and let her own works praise her in the gates.</u>" Proverbs 31: 27-31 (KJV)

"But if any provide not for his own, and specially for those of his own house, he hath denied the faith, and is worse than an infidel." 1 Timothy 5:8

"The desire of the slothful killeth him; for his hands refuse to labour." Proverbs 21:25 (KJV)

"As the door turneth upon his hinges, so doth the slothful upon his bed." Proverbs 26:14 (KJV)

"Slothfulness casteth into a deep sleep; and an idle soul shall suffer hunger." Proverbs 19:15 (KJV)

"By much slothfulness the building decayeth; and through idleness of the hands the house droppeth through." Ecclesiastes 10:18 (KJV)

⛶ Bottom line, God sees work as one way for a human to begin to become righteous. **Hard work is not the key to heaven, but one of the puzzle pieces of the true meaning of life.** Work hard, rest in due time, work honestly and don't overcharge for your services. This is a form of robbery and deceit.

🧩 Hard work doesn't

🧩 just happen. A lot of diligence goes into working hard. What is diligence? **<u>Diligence</u>:** Steady application in business of any kind; constant effort to accomplish what is undertaken; exertion of body or mind without unnecessary delay or sloth; due attention; industry; assiduity. (KJV Dictionary) **Diligence is also a puzzle piece of the true meaning of life.** In any situation, not just in the workplace, diligence is necessary. It is the drive to force yourself past doubt, obstacles, and lack of faith. It is not the "I think I can," it is the "I know I can, I will, and I will not give up." behind everything you do.

"Do thy diligence to come shortly unto me" 2 Timothy 4:9

"Keep thy heart with all diligence; for out of it are the issues of life." Proverbs 4:23

"Wherefore the rather, brethren, give diligence to make your calling and election sure: for if ye do these things, ye shall never fall" 2 Peter 1:10

"And we desire that every one of you do shew the same diligence to the full assurance of hope unto the end" Hebrews 6:11

"And beside this, giving all diligence, add to your faith virtue; and to virtue knowledge" 2 Peter 1:5

HOME

Home is a place where we should feel comfortable. After a long day at work, we get home and get comfy clothes on, eat familiar food, and let the weight of the world lift away— or maybe you have a different routine. Either way, when you walk in the door of home, it should feel like a relief from the outside world. Home should feel comfortable and safe and if it doesn't, then you need to find God and he will provide a safe home filled with all your needs. If you don't find God and you want to be immoral, you will be on your own. Good luck with that.

"And my people shall dwell in a peaceable habitation, and in sure dwellings, and in quiet resting places." Isaiah 32:18 (KJV)

"And into whatsoever house ye enter, first say, Peace be to this house." Luke 10:5 (KJV)

Some people go through life trying to conform to what they think other people expect them to be. Then when they get home, they are able to feel like themselves. Wherever you are, you should be living righteously—as according to the laws of God. **This is a puzzle piece to the true meaning of life. Righteousness.** Whether you are at home, at work, or at a store shopping, or making a social media video, God is observing your actions and thoughts. If you have a job that causes you to do immoral things in the eyes of God, then get home and read the bible—this is contradicting. It's a great start but your life should reflect the same moral standards no matter where you are. If you work in a church by daytime and at night, go act immorally, this is contradicting, too. If you try to conform to society and act immorally just to try to "fit in," then when you get home, you pray for forgiveness each and every day, you are imbalanced and need to fix it before it is too late.

Righteousness: Purity of heart and rectitude of life; conformity of heart and life to the divine law. (KJV Dictionary)

"But be ye doers of the word, and not hearers only, deceiving your own selves. For if any be a hearer of the word, and not a doer, he is like unto a man beholding his natural face in a glass: For he beholdeth himself, and goeth his way, and straightway forgetteth what manner of man he was." James 1:22-24 (KJV)

"A double minded man is unstable in all his ways." James 1:8 (KJV)

"The curse of the LORD is in the house of the wicked: but he blesseth the habitation of the just." Proverbs 3:33 (KJV)

"The labour of the righteous tendeth to life: the fruit of the wicked to sin." Proverbs 10:16 (KJV)

Some people think that once they get home and close the door, they are free to be anything because "it is their property and home, and they will do whatever they want." The door may be closed, and you may seem like you are in a private setting, but God sees everything and being home doesn't make the laws of

God diminish. The laws of God thrive no matter where you are and there are no walls or doors, or roofs that will ever be thick enough to hide your actions from God. If there is a lot of quarreling and negativity within the people of your home, it may be time to invite God into your home and all of the hearts that dwell within.

"And if a house be divided against itself, that house cannot stand." Mark 3:25 (KJV)

"Saying unto them, It is written, My house is the house of prayer: but ye have made it a den of thieves." Luke 19:46 (KJV)

"There is no darkness, nor shadow of death, where the workers of iniquity may hide themselves." Job 34:22 (KJV)

MARRIAGE

Marriage. Many people view marriage quite differently. Some people get married and divorced so much that it can be counted as their hobby. Other people view marriage as a current situation, knowing that divorce will save them should they ever get bored. Some people mean to stay married forever, but the other person in the relationship does something unforgettable. Other people view marriage as forever along with their spouses. Marriage is supposed to be forever, however even in the eyes of God, certain circumstances can cause forgivable divorces. Make sure when you say yes—that both of you have the same beliefs and are in it together forever. I've learned through the years that God will bless you and your spouse as long as you BOTH live for him.

Not every adult needs to get married. Marriage is a very special way of life, and it takes a lot of work for both people in the relationship. Marriage is meant for a man and a woman. Just because society is trying to push the "agenda" of LGBTQ (and any other letter people wish to identify as), it doesn't make it o.k. in God's eyes. Marriage was created by God so a man and a woman could come together as one and multiply society without being sexually immoral. God wants women to be submissive in a marriage and follow the husband's lead. God also wants the husband to honor their wives. It isn't a good idea to marry a person who doesn't believe in God, but if you are with a non-believer it is best to try to convert them.

"Thou shalt not lie with mankind, as with womankind: it is abomination." Leviticus 18:22

" Be ye not unequally yoked together with unbelievers: for what fellowship hath righteousness with unrighteousness? and what communion hath light with darkness?" 2 Corinthians 6:14

"Likewise, ye wives, be in subjection to your own husbands; that, if any obey not the word, they also may without the word be won by the conversation of the wives;" 1 Peter 3:1

"But to the rest speak I, not the Lord: If any brother a wife that believeth not, and she be pleased to dwell with him, let him not put her away. And the woman which hath an husband that believeth not, and if he be pleased to dwell with her, let her not leave him. For the unbelieving husband is sanctified by the wife, and the unbelieving wife is sanctified by the husband: else were

your children unclean; but now are they holy. But if the unbelieving depart, let him depart. A brother or a sister is not under bondage in such cases: but God hath called us to peace. For what knowest thou, O wife, whether thou shalt save thy husband? or how knowest thou, O man, whether thou shalt save thy wife?" 1 Corinthians 7:12-16

⛶ **Love is another key to the true meaning of life.** Without love, a marriage will fail—and a failed marriage will lead you to a bad place in God's eyes.

"Love is patient, love is kind. It does not envy, it does not boast, it is not proud. It does not dishonor others, it is not self-seeking, it is not easily angered, it keeps no record of wrongs. Love does not delight in evil but rejoices with the truth. It always protects, always trusts, always hopes, always perseveres. Love never fails." 1 Corinthians 13:4-8 (NIV)

If you don't think you can follow God's basic law for marriage (do not commit adultery), you would be better off not marrying. Marriage is a promise to God. It is better to not get married than to break a promise to God. Also, if you have a wandering eye and wish to see other people sexually, marriage isn't a good idea. If you like to "play the field, be warned—married or not, sexual misconduct is looked down upon greatly. This would be "going into" a woman whom you do not intend on taking as a wife—and if you are a woman, this would mean "taking a man inside you" whom you do not intend on taking as a husband.

"And if a man entice a maid that is not betrothed, and lie with her, he shall surely endow her to be his wife." Exodus 22:16 (KJV)

"Marriage is honourable in all, and the bed undefiled: but whoremongers and adulterers God will judge." Hebrews 13:4 (KJV)

"So then he that giveth her in marriage doeth well; but he that giveth her not in marriage doeth better." 1 Corinthians 7:38 (KJV)

"For a whore is a deep ditch; and a strange woman is a narrow pit." Proverbs 23:27 (KJV)

"Let the husband render unto the wife due benevolence: and likewise also the wife unto the husband." 1 Corinthians 7:3 (KJV)

"The wife hath not power of her own body, but the husband: and likewise also the husband hath not power of his own body, but the wife." 1 Corinthians 7:4 (KJV)

"And the contrary is in thee from other women in thy whoredoms, whereas none followeth thee to commit whoredoms: and in that thou givest a reward, and no reward is given unto thee, therefore thou art contrary. Wherefore, O harlot, hear the word of the LORD: Thus saith the Lord GOD; Because thy filthiness was poured out, and thy nakedness discovered through thy whoredoms with thy lovers, and with all the idols of thy abominations, and by the blood of thy children, which thou didst give unto them; Behold, therefore I will gather all thy lovers, with whom thou hast taken pleasure, and all them that thou hast loved, with all them that thou hast hated; I will even gather them round about against thee, and will discover thy nakedness unto them, that they may see all thy nakedness. And I will judge thee, as women that break wedlock and shed blood are judged; and I will give thee blood in fury and jealousy. And I will also give thee into their hand, and they shall throw down thine eminent place, and shall break down thy high places: they shall strip thee also of thy clothes, and shall take thy fair jewels, and leave thee naked and bare. They shall also bring up a company against thee, and they shall stone thee with stones, and

thrust thee through with their swords." Ezekiel 16:34-40 (KJV)

"Nevertheless let every one of you in particular so love his wife even as himself; and the wife see that she reverence her husband." Ephesians 5:33 (KJV)

Reverence is defined in the KJV dictionary as:

"To regard with fear mingled with respect and affection."

NOTE: Fear. Not fear for your life due to violence! Fear in the sense of loving someone so much that you have a hidden fear of losing him. Treating him as you want to be treated. Fear of him treating you how you treat him should you treat him badly or cheat. Fear of losing the love of your life and that fear should keep you committed to your promise to God and your wedding vows to your spouse.

PARENTING

Parenting is not for everyone. It involves a lot of love, a lot of patience, a lot of correction, a lot of time, a lot of sacrifice, a lot of teaching, and so much more. Some parents ignore their children, leaving only babysitters, themselves, or electronics to entertain them. This leads to a lot of future issues. Children have a lot of questions. If they do not have the proper guidance to get the answers, they will either go unanswered or be received from a questionable source—Either way, the result can be devastating.

Regarding the commandments:

"And these words, which I command thee this day, shall be in thine heart: And thou shalt teach them diligently unto thy children, and shalt talk of them when thou sittest in thine house, and when thou walkest by the way, and when thou liest down, and when thou risest up. And thou shalt bind them for a sign upon thine hand, and they shall be as frontlets between thine eyes. And thou shalt write them upon the posts of thy house, and on thy gates." Deuteronomy 6:6-9

Children need to be guided, corrected, and molded into the form they will ultimately be as an adult.   God wants us to teach our children all about the Trinity that is Him, Jesus, and the Holy Spirit. He wants the children to be brought up with discipline, correction, and the commandments as moral guidelines. Many parents are afraid to discipline. This is not ok. Everyone needs boundaries and consequences when boundaries are crossed. This is how people learn—adults and children.   It is up to the parents to set limits, consequences, and discipline, but balanced in love and God's word. Discipline doesn't hurt the child—not disciplining does hurt the child. Children won't be able to handle adult boundaries and laws if they are not made to handle them as kids.

"He that spareth his rod hateth his son: but he that loveth him chasteneth him betimes." Proverbs 13:24 (KJV)

"The rod and reproof give wisdom: but a child left to himself bringeth his mother to shame." Proverbs 29:15 (KJV)

"And all thy children shall be taught of the LORD; and great shall be the peace of thy children." Isaiah 54:13 (KJV)

Children are supposed to honor their father and mother, according to the 1st commandment. Well, in order for a child to honor their mother and father, the mother and father must first be honorable. If a mom is going to bars every night, or a dad is beating the mom, these are not honorable behaviors. These are just a couple examples of dishonorable behaviors—there are many more and you should be able to know right from wrong without listing all examples in this book.

God put this little life in your hands, and it is up to you to raise this child to be an honorable adult. If they choose to grow up and have their own kids, they will use everything you showed them and raise their kids according to God's ways. If you are not an honorable parent, they may still repeat your ways and pass those parenting techniques onto their children, but the result will not be honorable because the source was not honorable.

"Lo, children are an heritage of the LORD: and the fruit of the womb is his reward. As arrows are in the hand of a mighty man; so are children of the youth. Happy is the man that hath his quiver full of them: they shall not be ashamed, but they shall speak with the enemies in the gate." Psalm 127:3-5 (KJV)

Invite God into your heart and live for him in an honorable way—Then and only then can you pass on honorable acts to the child and be honored by the child and most importantly, God.

"Honour thy father and mother; (which is the first commandment with promise;)" Ephesians 6:2 (KJV)

"Train up a child in the way he should go: and when he is old, he will not depart from it." Proverbs 22:6 (KJV)

"My son, hear the instruction of thy father, and forsake not the law of thy mother: For they shall be an ornament of grace unto thy head, and chains about thy neck." Proverbs 1:8-9 (KJV)

"And, ye fathers, provoke not your children to wrath: but bring them up in the nurture and admonition of the Lord." Ephesians 6:4 (KJV)

🧩 **Being honorable is another puzzle piece to the true meaning of life.** According to the KJV dictionary, honorable is defined as, "Possessing a high mind; actuated by principles of honor, or a scrupulous regard to probity, rectitude or reputation."

Being an honorable person in all situations is important and leads to righteousness, good deeds, and honoring God.

"A man's pride shall bring him low: but honour shall uphold the humble in spirit." Proverbs 29:23 (KJV)

"Let my mouth be filled with thy praise and with thy honour all the day." Proverbs 71:8 (KJV)

"He that followeth after righteousness and mercy findeth life, righteousness, and honour." Proverbs 21:21(KJV)

If you are a dishonorable parent, there is still hope for your child. If they find God and receive Him in their heart, they will be brought to honorable actions by God—The Father of all. Parenting is ultimately up to the parents, though.

"When my father and my mother forsake me, then the LORD will take me up." Psalm 27:10 (KJV)

CHILDLESS LIFE

Becoming a parent is a huge decision and commitment. If you don't think you want kids, then you shouldn't have them. It is okay to not have kids. Even if you feel like society "looks down" on you because you don't have kids, it is a personal decision that doesn't have to be explained to anyone. It is better to remain childless than have kids and not properly parent them. It isn't society's choice—this choice is between you and God.

"Better it is to have no children, and to have virtue: for the memorial thereof is immortal: because it is known with God, and with men." Wisdom of Solomon 4:1 (KJV)

"For, behold, the days are coming, in the which they shall say, Blessed are the barren, and the wombs that never bare, and the paps which never gave suck." Luke 23:29 (KJV)

If you unexpectedly become pregnant and don't want kids, it is better to have the baby and give it up for adoption through a trustworthy agency than it is to abort. No matter how you feel about it, your body is God's temple and the "my body my choice" excuse is invalidated by the bible. Abortion is murder and unless you want murder on your sin list, it is recommended to give that baby a chance at life and place it up for adoption.

"Thou shalt not kill." Exodus 20:13 (KJV)

"And he that killeth any man shall surely be put to death." Leviticus 24:17 (KJV)

"What? know ye not that your body is the temple of the Holy Ghost which is in you, which ye have of God, and ye are not your own?" 1 Corinthians 6:19 (KJV)

"According as he hath chosen us in him before the foundation of the world, that we should be holy and without blame before him in love: Having predestinated us unto the adoption of children by Jesus Christ to himself, according to the good pleasure of his will" Ephesians 1:4-5

Upon conception, a human is formed in the womb. This tiny human is a gift from God that is the temple of God, and it contains the Holy Spirit. Tiny but mighty, a form of God is inside you. Nurture this gift and if you wish to give it up, at least do so in the form of life, not destruction and death.

"As thou knowest not what is the way of the spirit, nor how the bones do grow in the womb of her that is with child: even so thou knowest not the works of God who maketh all." Ecclesiastes 11:5 (KJV)

"Before I formed thee in the belly I knew thee; and before thou camest forth out of the womb I sanctified thee, and I ordained thee a prophet unto the nations." Jeremiah 1:5 (KJV)

"Your eyes saw my unformed substance; in your book were written, every one of them, the days that were formed for me, when as yet there was none of them." Psalm 139:16 (ESV)

"For he shall be great in the sight of the Lord, and shall drink neither wine nor strong drink; and he shall be filled with the Holy Ghost, even from his mother's womb." Luke 1:15 (KJV)

"Lo, children are an heritage of the LORD: and the fruit of the womb is his reward." Psalms 127:3 (KJV)

"If men strive, and hurt a woman with child, so that her fruit depart from her, and yet no mischief follow: he shall be surely punished, according as the woman's husband will lay upon him; and he shall pay

as the judges determine. And if any mischief follow, then thou shalt give life for life, Eye for eye, tooth for tooth, hand for hand, foot for foot, Burning for burning, wound for wound, stripe for stripe. " Exodus 21:22 (KJV)

When a woman who does not want kids finds out she is pregnant, she has to decide what to do. **A big puzzle piece of the true meaning of life is integrity**. **Integrity** is defined as,

"The entire, unimpaired state of any thing, particularly of the mind; moral soundness or purity; incorruptness; uprightness; honesty. integrity comprehends the whole moral character…." (Webster 1828) ***Also known as doing the right thing even when nobody is looking.***

In this situation, many women run to a clinic and have an abortion and keep it a secret. They think what isn't seen didn't happen. Although they feel ashamed, they still complete the act. Integrity means doing the right thing—even if other people don't know. The right thing isn't necessarily society approved, but it is always God approved. God says murder is bad. God says life in the womb has a soul. So, having integrity would be having the baby and giving it a chance at life, even if it means giving it up for adoption. That baby is a very wanted gift for many couples who cannot conceive.

"But as for me, I will walk in mine integrity: redeem me, and be merciful unto me." Psalm 26:11

"The LORD shall judge the people: judge me, O LORD, according to my righteousness, and according to mine integrity that is in me." Psalms 7:8

"So he fed them according to the integrity of his heart; and guided them by the skillfulness of his hands." Psalm 78:72

"The integrity of the upright shall guide them: but the perverseness of transgressors shall destroy them." Proverbs 11:3

If you are single and not planning on starting a family, don't be sexually active. (See Single Life Section of this book) If you are married and are not interested in starting a family, use birth control. It is better to prevent a pregnancy than it is to end one.

SINGLE LIFE

Not all adults are meant to be married. It is o.k. to stay single for your entire life. It is not acceptable in God's eyes to have sex if you are single, though. If you want to remain single and have sex with numerous people, you are being sexually immoral in God's eyes and performing sins against his body (which is the Temple of God).

Abstain from the desires of the flesh, the sinful lusts, and immoral sexual thoughts. Single people are supposed to live holy like Jesus. Marriage was created to fulfill sexual desires in a moral fashion. If you have sex with another human, God considers you married to them.

"What? know ye not that he which is joined to an harlot is one body? for two, saith he, shall be one flesh." 1 Corinthians 6:16 (KJV) Any sex with another person after that is adultery, which is a commandment thou shall not break. **Abstinence is a puzzle piece for the true meaning of life.** Abstinence in this sense is from sex, but as a puzzle piece to the true meaning of life, it is to refrain from any sinful act. Abstaining from sin is a difficult task. We as humans were born to sin. Just do your best, work hard at it, and build up

your strength to decline bad actions. Some small sins will probably still occur, just ask for forgiveness each day, and build your relationship with God and he will give you strength.

Abstinence: The refraining from an indulgence of appetite, or from customary gratifications of animal propensities. (Websters 1828)

"For I would that all men were even as I myself. But every man hath his proper gift of God, one after this manner, and another after that. I say therefore to the unmarried and widows, It is good for them if they abide even as I. But if they cannot contain, let them marry: for it is better to marry than to burn." 1 Corinthians 7:7-9 (KJV)

"Flee fornication. Every sin that a man doeth is without the body; but he that committeth fornication sinneth against his own body." 1 Corinthians 6:18 (KJV)

"There is difference also between a wife and a virgin. The unmarried woman careth for the things of the Lord, that she may be holy both in body and in spirit: but she that is married careth for the things of the world, how she may please her husband." 1 Corinthians 7:34 (KJV)

"Now concerning the things whereof ye wrote unto me: It is good for a man not to touch a woman. Nevertheless, to avoid fornication, let every man have his own wife, and let every woman have her own husband." 1 Corinthian 7:1-2 (KJV)

"Know ye not that the unrighteous shall not inherit the kingdom of God? Be not deceived: neither fornicators, nor idolaters, nor adulterers, nor effeminate, nor abusers of themselves with mankind, Nor thieves, nor covetous, nor drunkards, nor revilers, nor extortioners, shall inherit the kingdom of God." 1 Corinthians 6:9-10 (KJV)

In order to abstain from sin, you must be able to portray Godliness. **Godliness is a necessary puzzle piece to the true meaning of life.** Godliness is, "A religious life; a careful observance of the laws of God and performance of religious duties, proceeding from love and reverence for the divine character and commands; Christian obedience."

It is impossible to sin and live in Godliness. Living Godly means finding all the keys to the true meaning of life and using them each and every day.

"But thou, O man of God, flee these things; and follow after righteousness, godliness, faith, love, patience, meekness." 1 Timothy 6:11 (KJV)

"For bodily exercise profiteth little: but godliness is profitable unto all things, having promise of the life that now is, and of that which is to come." 1 Timothy 4:8 (KJV)

"According as his divine power hath given unto us all things that pertain unto life and godliness, through the knowledge of him that hath called us to glory and virtue" 2 Peter 1:3 (KJV)

SEXUAL CONDUCT

No it is NOT o.k. to be gay, according to God.

Society tries to make up their own rules as they go. They shame the people who feel uncomfortable around gay behavior, or who states it is against their religion. The people who don't accept the "LGBTQ community" are shamed and called homo-phobes and other obnoxious names. This is not o.k. in the eyes of God. People of God know it is better to be called a name for obeying God's words than to be accept it and sin against God, though. I am not a "homo-phobe" for writing this. I am just a messenger. I don't fear gay people, I fear God. I am not saying God will throw all gay people in Hell. I am saying, in order to completely live for God, you must follow all of God's laws. You can love God and be gay, but you can't give your soul to Him when fulfilling your own desires instead of His.

"Thou shalt not lie with mankind, as with womankind: it is abomination." Leviticus 18:22 (KJV)

"An unjust man is an abomination to the just: and he that is upright in the way is abomination to the wicked." Proverbs 29:27 (KJV)

The media throws in gay acts constantly. Even kids shows put on Dis+ portray questionable acts. Trying to normalize an abomination to God does not ever make the action acceptable. Trying to teach kids it is o.k. to go against God's actions is not acceptable, either. Even commercials show drag queens, gay couples, and gay acts now. You can't go anywhere without the devil aiming his beliefs at your face. Do what you will. Watch what you will. However, God is not approving of anything involving cross dressing, L, G, B, T, or Q! This action, although normalized in society, is not of God--but an evil temptation from Satan himself, trying to pull you away from the word of God.

"If a man also lie with mankind, as he lieth with a woman, both of them have committed an abomination: they shall surely be put to death; their blood shall be upon them." Leviticus 20:13 (KJV)

God does not want women to dress like men, or men to dress like women. God does not want a woman to "identify" as a man or a man to "identify" as a woman, animal, tree, or anything other than what God made them. You don't choose a gender. God chose your gender prior to your birth. You can't change God's work. It isn't your body; it is HIS TEMPLE. You can't let your child choose their gender. This is not a choice for a child, but for GOD—and he already chose when he put that little soul in your womb.

"So God created man in his own image, in the image of God created he him; male and female created he them." Genesis 1:27

"The woman shall not wear that which pertaineth unto a man, neither shall a man put on a woman's garment: for all that do so are abomination unto the LORD thy God." Deuteronomy 22:5 (KJV)

" Know ye not that ye are the temple of God, and that the Spirit of God dwelleth in you?" 1 Corinthians 3:16 (KJV)

"Know ye not that the unrighteous shall not inherit the kingdom of God? Be not deceived: neither fornicators, nor idolaters, nor adulterers, <u>nor effeminate</u>, nor abusers of themselves with mankind, Nor thieves, nor covetous, nor drunkards, nor revilers, nor extortioners, shall inherit the kingdom of God." 1 Corinthians 6:9-10 (KJV)

Effeminate is defined by the KJV dictionary as: 1. Having the qualities of the female sex; soft or delicate to an unmanly degree; tender; womanish; voluptuous.

Gay marriage doesn't make gay sexual conduct o.k. either. God only accepts marriages between a man and a woman. So gay sexual action is accepted in God's eyes.

"Therefore shall a man leave his father and his mother, and shall cleave unto his wife: and they shall be one flesh." Genesis 2:24 (KJV)

"Nevertheless, to avoid fornication, let every man have his own wife, and let every woman have her own husband." 1 Corinthians 7:2 (KJV)

"Wherefore God also gave them up to uncleanness through the lusts of their own hearts, to dishonour their own bodies between themselves: Who changed the truth of God into a lie, and worshipped and served the creature more than the Creator, who is blessed for ever. Amen. For this cause God gave them up unto vile affections: ***for even their women did change the natural use into that which is against nature: And likewise also the men, leaving the natural use of the woman, burned in their lust one toward another; men with men working that which is unseemly, and receiving in themselves that***

__recompence of their error which was meet__. And even as they did not like to retain God in their knowledge, God gave them over to a reprobate mind, to do those things which are not convenient; Being filled with all unrighteousness, __fornication__, wickedness, covetousness, maliciousness; full of envy, murder, debate, deceit, malignity; whisperers, Backbiters, haters of God, despiteful, __proud__, boasters, inventors of evil things, disobedient to parents, Without understanding, covenantbreakers, __without natural affection__, implacable, unmerciful: __Who knowing the judgment of God, that they which commit such things are worthy of death, not only do the same, but have pleasure in them that do them.__ " Romans 1:24-32 (KJV)

As for straight people—see Single Life section for more sexual conduct information, regarding non-gay acts.

"But if they cannot contain, let them marry: for it is better to marry than to burn. 1 Corinthians 7:9(KJV)

☖ **Being humble and full of humility is a puzzle piece to the true meaning of life.** Pride is not good. Pride is a sin and enforcing one of God's abominations is definitely a smack in God's face. Creating a huge "Gay Pride" agenda in society does not make it any less of a sin. Live humble in all means and show humility to God. Giving people extra rights and honors in life due to LGBTQ is a sin. Showing "Gay Pride" flags all over is probably not a good idea, either. *"He that justifieth the wicked, and he that condemneth the just, even they both are abomination to the LORD."* Proverbs 17:15 (KJV)

Pride is "an unreasonable conceit of one's own superiority in talents, beauty, wealth, accomplishments, rank or elevation in office, which manifests itself in lofty airs, distance, reserve, and often in contempt of others." (KJV Dictionary)

Humble, according to the KJV dictionary is: "In an evangelical sense, having a low opinion of one's self, and a deep sense of unworthiness in the sight of God."

Humility is: "freedom from pride and arrogance; humbleness of mind; a modest estimate of one's own worth; In theology, humility consists in lowliness of mind; a deep sense of one's own unworthiness in the sight of God, self-abasement, penitence for sin, and submission to the divine will." (KJV Dictionary)

"A man's pride shall bring him low: but honour shall uphold the humble in spirit." Proverbs 29:23

"When pride cometh, then cometh shame: but with the lowly is wisdom." Proverbs 11:2 (KJV)

"Better it is to be of an humble spirit with the lowly, than to divide the spoil with the proud." Proverbs 16:12 (KJV)

"Humble yourselves in the sight of the Lord, and he shall lift you up." James 4:10 (KJV)

"Do ye think that the scripture saith in vain, The spirit that dwelleth in us lusteth to envy? But he giveth more grace. Wherefore he saith, God resisteth the proud, but giveth grace unto the humble." James 4:5-6 (KJV)

"Let nothing be done through strife or vainglory; but in lowliness of mind let each esteem other better than themselves." Philippians 2:3 (KJV)

"For from within, out of the heart of men, proceed evil thoughts, adulteries, fornications, murders, Thefts, covetousness, wickedness, deceit, lasciviousness, an evil eye, blasphemy, **pride,** *foolishness: All these evil things come from within, and defile the man."* Mark 7:21-23 (KJV)

FRIENDSHIP

Friendships vary considerably among different groups of people. Some people have large circles of friends, but barely know them individually. Some people have 1 really close friend, and they would do anything for them. Other people use people for convenient things they receive from them but are only there in a limited way for them. Some people call all their social media followers "friends."

Many of those people that are called "friends" should really be called acquaintances, frenemies, enemies, traitors, exploiters, and trouble….but not true friends. Friends can be good or bad according to God. You are who you hang out with, so be warned if your friends are fond of evil acts—you will be associated with those acts as well. If you are calling frenemies, enemies, exploiters, traitors, and people who cause trouble your friends, you may want to reevaluate your "friendships". Each word is defined below. Compare the definition to certain people in your life's actions and decide whether they are worthy of being called "friend."

"Make no friendship with an angry man; and with a furious man thou shalt not go" Proverbs 22:24 (KJV)

"He that walketh with wise men shall be wise: but a companion of fools shall be destroyed." Proverbs 13:20 (KJV)

"He that justifieth the wicked, and he that condemneth the just, even they both are abomination to the LORD." Proverbs 17:15 (KJV)

"Let love be without dissimulation. Abhor that which is evil; cleave to that which is good." Romans 12:9 (KJV)

<u>Friend</u>: One who is attached to another by affection; one who entertains for another sentiments of esteem, respect, and affection, which lead him to desire his company, and to seek to promote his happiness and prosperity; opposed to foe or enemy. (KJV Dictionary)

<u>Acquaintance</u>: Familiar knowledge; a state of being acquainted, or of having intimate or more than slight or superficial knowledge; (KJV Dictionary)

<u>Frenemy</u>: A person who is or pretends to be a friend but who is also in some ways an enemy or rival (Merriam-Webster)

Enemy: A foe; an adversary. A private enemy is one who hates another and wishes him injury, or attempts to do him injury to gratify his own malice or ill will. (KJV Dictionary)

Traitor: One who betrays his trust. (KJV Dictionary)

Exploiter: 1. In a ludicrous sense, a great act of wickedness. (KJV Dictionary)

2. to make use of meanly or unfairly for one's own advantage (Merriam-Webster)

A true friend will always be there for you. Those are the people in your life who you should keep associating with. The rest are best left behind. If people in your life only cause you grief and bad will, you shouldn't allow them in your life anymore.

"Greater love hath no man than this, that a man lay down his life for his friends." John 15:13 (KJV)

Not everyone is your friend, so God gives us a warning:

"For he knew who should betray him; therefore said he, Ye are not all clean." John 13:11 (KJV)

"A friend loveth at all times, and a brother is born for adversity." Proverbs 17:17 (KJV)

Never treat an enemy in a revengeful way. Always treat others as you want them to treat you. If they are mean, return their actions with kindness otherwise you will be no different than them and your actions will be identical to the qualities that make them your enemy.

"If thou meet thine enemy's ox or his ass going astray, thou shalt surely bring it back to him again." Exodus 23:4 (KJV)

It is better to walk away or perform a kind act than retaliate.

"Recompense to no man evil for evil. Provide things honest in the sight of all men. If it be possible, as much as lieth in you, live peaceably with all men. Dearly beloved, avenge not yourselves, but rather give place unto wrath: for it is written, Vengeance is mine; I will repay, saith the Lord." Romans 12:17-19 (KJV)

"Therefore if thine enemy hunger, feed him; if he thirst, give him drink: for in so doing thou shalt heap coals of fire on his head. Be not overcome of evil, but overcome evil with good." Romans 12:20-21 (KJV)

It is absolutely necessary to use discretion when choosing your friends. **Using discretion is a puzzle piece to the true meaning of life.** Discretion needs to be used when making any decision in life, in order to stay on the road to righteousness and living for God.

<u>**Discretion**</u>: "Prudence, or knowledge and prudence; that discernment which enables a person to judge critically of what is correct and proper, united with caution; nice discernment and judgment, directed by circumspection, and primarily regarding one's own conduct." (KJV Dictionary)

"A good man sheweth favour, and lendeth: he will guide his affairs with discretion." Psalms 112:5 (KJV)

"Discretion shall preserve thee, understanding shall keep thee." Proverbs 2:11 (KJV)

CHARITY

⚙ **C**harity is an act of love toward others, and a **puzzle piece to the true meaning of life.** God wants us to give unto others. We are put here to help others overcome life and find God in the end. Charitable acts show others the miracle of God and give the recipient hope and faith in something more than the stresses they are facing on Earth.

If you read various versions of the Holy Bible (KJV, NIV, Geneva, etc.), you will realize that the words charity and love are used in the same verses to replace one another. That is because according to the KJV dictionary, "In a theological sense, it (charity) includes supreme love to God, and universal good will to men." You can have charity without love, but you can't have love without charity.

Charity: In a general sense, love, benevolence, good will; that disposition of heart which inclines men to think favorably of their fellow men to think favorably of their fellow men, and to do them good….Liberality to the poor, consisting in almsgiving or benefactions, or in gratuitous services to relieve them in distress. (KJV Dictionary)

<u>Alms</u>: Anything given gratuitously to relieve the poor, as money, food, or clothing, otherwise called charity. (KJV Dictionary)

"Take heed that ye do not your alms before men, to be seen of them: otherwise ye have no reward of your Father which is in heaven." Matthew 6:1 (KJV)

<u>Benefaction</u>: Donation or gift (Merriam-Webster)

"And though I have the gift of prophecy, and understand all mysteries, and all knowledge; and though I have all faith, so that I could remove mountains, and have not charity, I am nothing." 1 Corinthians 13:2 (KJV)

God forgives us through charitable acts toward others. Don't think you can be mean to everyone around you, then give $50 to a charity and be forgiven of all your sins. Being charitable isn't just a $ donation. It is a way of life. To seek those in need and help in any way you can. Charity given in love is returned to you in the future. Give unselfishly and for the right reasons, and you will receive rewards from God.

"And above all things have fervent charity among yourselves: for charity shall cover the multitude of sins." 1 Peter 4:8 (KJV)

"But rather give alms of such things as ye have; and, behold, all things are clean unto you." Luke 11:41 (KJV)

"Every man according as he purposeth in his heart, so let him give; not grudgingly, or of necessity: for God loveth a cheerful giver." 2 Corinthians 9:7 (KJV)

"Give, and it shall be given unto you; good measure, pressed down, and shaken together, and running over, shall men give into your bosom. For with the same measure that ye mete withal it shall be measured to you again." Luke 6:38 (KJV)

Help people in need without telling the world on social media. If you have to announce your givings, you are probably giving for the wrong reason (selfish attention). God wants you to give quietly. All that matters is the person is helped. God knows you helped, and it is noted.

"That thine alms may be in secret: and thy Father which seeth in secret himself shall reward thee openly." Matthew 6:4 (KJV)

"Take heed that ye do not your alms before men, to be seen of them: otherwise ye have no reward of your Father which is in heaven." Matthew 6:1 (KJV)

"But when thou doest alms, let not thy left hand know what thy right hand doeth." Matthew 6:3 (KJV)

We are supposed to share our wealth with those who are in need. Even if you feel you may be struggling, take a closer look and see how much you truly have to give. Charity lies not only in money, but in time, gifts from the heart, attention, and love. Your earthly treasures collect dust and are truly worthless in the big picture. Your heavenly treasures are the rewards you receive in heaven for the true and righteous actions on Earth.

"But lay up for yourselves treasures in heaven, where neither moth nor rust doth corrupt, and where thieves do not break through nor steal" Matthew 6:20 (KJV)

"Sell that ye have, and give alms; provide yourselves bags which wax not old, a treasure in the heavens that faileth not, where no thief approacheth, neither moth corrupteth." Luke 12:33 (KJV)

In summary, we are put here to do works of God on Earth. Love one another, help one another.

"Whoso stoppeth his ears at the cry of the poor, he also shall cry himself, but shall not be heard." Proverbs 21:13 (KJV)

"He that hath a bountiful eye shall be blessed; for he giveth of his bread to the poor." Proverbs 22:9 (KJV)

"Give to him that asketh thee, and from him that would borrow of thee turn not thou away." Matthew 5:42 (KJV)

"Withhold not good from them to whom it is due, when it is in the power of thine hand to do it." Proverbs 3:27 (KJV)

"I have shewed you all things, how that so labouring ye ought to support the weak, and to remember the words of the Lord Jesus, how he said, It is more blessed to give than to receive." Acts 20:35 (KJV)

Charity is an act of love and brotherly kindness. Kindness can be defined as a genuine concern for another. In order to give charity from the heart, you must have love and a genuine concern for the recipient(s) of your charitable act. **Kindness is definitely a puzzle piece to the true meaning of life.** Genuine concern for others is required to feel love and provide true charity.

"The desire of a man is his kindness: and a poor man is better than a liar." Proverbs 19:22 (KJV)

"She openeth her mouth with wisdom; and in her tongue is the law of kindness." Proverbs 31:26 (KJV)

"In a little wrath I hid my face from thee for a moment; but with everlasting kindness will I have mercy on thee, saith the LORD thy Redeemer." Isaiah 54:8 (KJV)

"That in the ages to come he might shew the exceeding riches of his grace in his kindness toward us through Christ Jesus." Ephesians 2:7 (KJV)

"For the mountains shall depart, and the hills be removed; but my kindness shall not depart from thee, neither shall the covenant of my peace be removed, saith the LORD that hath mercy on thee." Isaiah 54:10 (KJV)

IMAGE

Everyone has an image. Image is a full picture of how you portray yourself to others, and it includes the way you look, smell, dress, and act. It is important that the image you portray to others matches the image you portray to God. For instance, a person who pretends to be holy to others and acts revengeful behind closed doors is portraying a false image to society, but God sees and know everything. Also, what good is a priest—who dedicates their life to God if he is sinning behind closed doors? Sinful acts behind closed doors are not part of the image you are portraying to society, but they are part of the image you are portraying to God. Being a man during the day and dressing like a woman at night is a lie. You can walk around and act perfect all you want. You can fool everyone around you—but the most important thing to remember is this—in the big picture of life, those people you are trying to impress mean nothing. You can't have eternal life if you don't impress God.

"And as we have borne the image of the earthy, we shall also bear the image of the heavenly." 1 Corinthians 15:49 (KJV)

"For a man indeed ought not to cover his head, forasmuch as he is the image and glory of God: but the woman is the glory of the man." 1 Corinthians 11:7 (KJV)

"The words of his mouth were smoother than butter, but war was in his heart: his words were softer than oil, yet were they drawn swords." Psalms 55:21 (KJV)

"The woman shall not wear that which pertaineth unto a man, neither shall a man put on a woman's garment: for all that do so are abomination unto the LORD thy God." Deuteronomy 22:5 (KJV)

"If any man among you seem to be religious, and bridleth not his tongue, but deceiveth his own heart, this man's religion is vain." James 1:26 (KJV)

Purity is a puzzle piece to the true meaning of life. How can a person be pure if they act differently around different people? Maybe you are confused about what purity means.

Purity: 1. Freedom from foreign admixture or heterogeneous matter; as the purity of water, of wine, of spirit; the purity of drugs; the purity of metals. 2. Cleanness; freedom from foulness or dirt; as the purity of a garment. 3. Freedom from guilt or the defilement of sin; innocence; as purity of heart or life. (KJV Dictionary)

You cannot be pure if your image is not true. Think about it. You are mixing a pure image with secret sinful acts. If you buy an essential oil, you know if it says 100% pure, that it only contains 100% of the only stated on that bottle. Something can only be pure if it is not mixed with other things. If you want to be 100% pure for God, then you cannot pretend to be a Godly person and break commandments behind the scenes. Purity has to match inside and out and not be mixed with other ways.

"Blessed are the pure in heart: for they shall see God." Matthew 5:8 (KJV)

"Unto the pure all things are pure: but unto them that are defiled and unbelieving is nothing pure; but even their mind and conscience is defiled." Titus 1:15 (KJV)

" Not every one that saith unto me, Lord, Lord, shall enter into the kingdom of heaven; but he that doeth the will of my Father which is in heaven. Many will say to me in that day, Lord, Lord, have we not prophesied in thy name? and in thy name have cast out devils? and in thy name done many wonderful works? And

then will I profess unto them, I never knew you: depart from me, ye that work iniquity." Matthew 7:21-23 (KJV)

"Lay hands suddenly on no man, neither be partaker of other men's sins: keep thyself pure." 1 Timothy 5:22 (KJV)

"The way of man is froward and strange: but as for the pure, his work is right." Proverbs *21:8 (KJV)*

"There is a generation that are pure in their own eyes, and yet is not washed from their filthiness." Proverbs 30:12 (KJV)

"He that hath clean hands, and a pure heart; who hath not lifted up his soul unto vanity, nor sworn deceitfully. He shall receive the blessing from the LORD, and righteousness from the God of his salvation." Psalms 24:4-5 (KJV)

FAITH & VIRTUE

Faith is defined by the KJV bible dictionary as,

"The judgment that what another states or testifies is the truth."

It can be difficult to believe in things beyond your visual capabilities. **Faith is a puzzle piece to the true meaning of life.** Without faith, you do not have God in your heart, or the belief in the Trinity. Without this, you cannot possibly obtain the true meaning of life. You have to have faith. All it takes is a tiny bit. Faith is like a mustard seed. A mustard seed begins as a speck and grows into a huge tree-like plant that keeps producing. Faith begins as a speck and grows into a huge fulfilling vine of emotional nourishment. Believe that God is on your side and will provide for you in any time of trouble—all things you need will be given if you ask and believe.

"And all things, whatsoever ye shall ask in prayer, believing, ye shall receive." Matthew 21:22 (KJV)

"But let him ask in faith, nothing wavering. For he that wavereth is like a wave of the sea driven with the wind and tossed." James 1:6 (KJV)

" Jesus said unto them, Because of your unbelief: for verily I say unto you, If ye have faith as a grain of mustard seed, ye shall say unto this mountain, Remove hence to yonder place; and it shall remove; and nothing shall be impossible unto you." Matthew 17:20 (KJV)

Remember the Loaves and Fishes Story? There were 5,000 men, 5 loaves of bread and 2 fish. The disciples depended on God to provide the right amount of food for a very large group when they only had the visual amount for a small group. The disciples believed in and relied on God and God provided—with extra left over.

Jesus said, *"Give ye them to eat."* *"And they said, We have no more but five loaves and two fishes; except we should go and buy meat for all this people. For they were about five thousand men. And he said to his disciples, Make them sit down by fifties in a company. And they did so, and made them all sit down. Then he took the five loaves and the two fishes, and looking up to heaven, he blessed them, and brake, and gave to the disciples to set before the multitude. And they did eat, and were all filled: and there was taken up of fragments that remained to them twelve baskets."* Luke 9:16 (KJV)

⛶ Faith means nothing if you don't add virtue to it. Virtue is defined as strength and bravery (KJV Dictionary).   If you don't have the bravery to show others or the strength to keep your faith, even in the toughest of times, then faith becomes temporary. Virtue must accompany faith—because of this, **Virtue is another puzzle piece to the true meaning of life.**

"According as his divine power hath given unto us all things that pertain unto life and godliness, through the knowledge of him that hath called us to glory and virtue" 2 Peter 1:3 (KJV)

"Finally, brethren, whatsoever things are true, whatsoever things are honest, whatsoever things are just, whatsoever things are pure, whatsoever things are lovely, whatsoever things are of good report; if there be any virtue, and if there be any praise, think on these things." Philippians 4:8 (KJV)

"Who can find a virtuous woman? for her price is far above rubies." Proverbs 31:10 (KJV)

"A virtuous woman is a crown to her husband: but she that maketh ashamed is as rottenness in his bones." Proverbs 12:4 (KJV)

SOCIETY

Everyone seems to copy each other pretty easily. It seems the "If the majority is doing it, it must be right." mentality is at an all-time high. Did you know that the majority isn't always right? It doesn't take strength to follow all the other people's actions.

"Thou shalt not follow a multitude to do evil; neither shalt thou speak in a cause to decline after many to wrest judgment" Exodus 23:2 (KJV)

"And be not conformed to this world: but be ye transformed by the renewing of your mind, that ye may prove what is that good, and acceptable, and perfect, will of God." Romans 12:2 (KJV)

People take the easy way out. They know they will blend in if they do what everyone else is doing. They think it will lead them to instant acceptance. O.k. society accepts you. Now what? Good job. Now you will be grouped with the rest of the sinners in the world, according to God.

We all sin. I get it. Nobody is perfect. The important thing is you ask for forgiveness, don't repeat the offense, and live for God to the best of your ability. Living for God means you don't copy society. It means you stand up for what is right in God's eyes, even if it is wrong in the eyes of society.

"Blessed is the man that walketh not in the counsel of the ungodly, nor standeth in the way of sinners, nor sitteth in the seat of the scornful." Psalms 1:1 (KJV)

Constantly being accepting of what society is jamming down your throat is not what God wants us to do. Before accepting anything as "the right way," read the bible and open your eyes to what "the right way" is.

"Beloved, believe not every spirit, but try the spirits whether they are of God: because many false prophets are gone out into the world." 1 John 4:1 (KJV)

God does not want us to accept everyone. There are certain acts that are an abomination to God. These acts are accepted by society and those who follow God, don't accept the acts and society calls us names. It is o.k. to go against society. God know you are not in the wrong in this situation and that is all that matters.

"Fret not thyself because of evildoers, neither be thou envious against the workers of

iniquity. For they shall soon be cut down like the grass, and wither as the green herb. Trust in the LORD, and do good; so shalt thou dwell in the land, and verily thou shalt be fed. Delight thyself also in the LORD; and he shall give thee the desires of thine heart. Commit thy way unto the LORD; trust also in him; and he shall bring it to pass. And he shall bring forth thy righteousness as the light, and thy judgment as the noonday. Rest in the LORD, and wait patiently for him: fret not thyself because of him who prospereth in his way, because of the man who bringeth wicked devices to pass. " Psalm 37:1-7 (KJV)

"Behold, I give unto you power to tread on serpents and scorpions, and over all the power of the enemy: and nothing shall by any means hurt you." Luke 10:19 (KJV)

"Beloved, believe not every spirit, but try the spirits whether they are of God: because many false prophets are gone out into the world. " 1 John 4:1 (KJV)

"Ye adulterers and adulteresses, know ye not that the friendship of the world is enmity with God? whosoever therefore will be a friend of the world is the enemy of God. " James 4:4 (KJV)

"For the grace of God that bringeth salvation hath appeared to all men, Teaching us that, denying ungodliness and worldly lusts, we should live soberly, righteously, and godly, in this present world;" Titus 2:11-12 (KJV)

It is important that you know the difference between what is good and what is evil in the eyes of God. To do this, you need knowledge. **Knowledge is another puzzle piece to the true meaning of life**, and it is defined as, " A clear and certain perception of that which exists, or of truth and fact" (KJV Dictionary). Knowledge will give you the ability to live the right way. Be careful, though. Once you have the knowledge to know better, you must do better. Combine the faith in God with Virtue (strength) and knowledge (to know better) and you will be on the right path to living for God.   You can have faith in God, but without virtue and knowledge, that faith doesn't last.

"And beside this, giving all diligence, add to your faith virtue; and to virtue knowledge" 2 Peter 1:5 (KJV)

"The heart of the prudent getteth knowledge; and the ear of the wise seeketh knowledge." Proverbs 18:15 (KJV)

"My people are destroyed for lack of knowledge: because thou hast rejected knowledge, I will also reject thee, that thou shalt be no priest to me: seeing thou hast forgotten the law of thy God, I will also forget thy children." Hosea 4:6 (KJV)

"Who is this that darkeneth counsel by words without knowledge?" Job 38:2 (KJV)

"Whereby, when ye read, ye may understand my knowledge in the mystery of Christ." Ephesians 3:4 (KJV)

"A wise man is strong; yea, a man of knowledge increaseth strength." Proverbs 24:5 (KJV)

"Receive my instruction, and not silver; and knowledge rather than choice gold." Proverbs 8:10 (KJV)

Did you know you either love God or the worldly ways, not both? That's right. It is time to make a choice and to stand up for the right way, even if it makes you a minority.

"Love not the world, neither the things that are in the world. If any man love the world, the love of the Father is not in him." 1 John 2:15 (KJV)

"For what shall it profit a man, if he shall gain the whole world, and lose his own soul?" Mark 8:36 (KJV)

"Beloved, follow not that which is evil, but that which is good. He that doeth good is of God: but he that doeth evil hath not seen God." 3 John 1:11 (KJV)

"For the grace of God that bringeth salvation hath appeared to all men, Teaching us that, denying ungodliness and worldly lusts, we should live soberly, righteously, and godly, in this present world;" Titus 2:11-12 (KJV)

Be committed to God in everything you do. **Commitment to God is a puzzle piece in the true meaning of life.** Without being committed to God, you can't obtain all the other puzzle pieces. If you aren't committed to God, then you won't have the will to live for him, and your puzzle will be nonexistent.

Do everything with prayer and good intentions and the correct path will be shown to you by God. Commit yourself to God and he will get you through anything, including the evil words thrown your way when you turn your back on the sins of society. The good is still the majority. The problem is the media shows only the bad. Look for good people and you will find them. Form strong groups and help others become part of God's society. The Earthly societies are full of evil and deceit.

Commit, according to the KJV dictionary, is defined as: Literally, to send to or upon; to throw, put or lay upon. Hence, to give in trust; to put into the hands or power of another; to entrust; with to.

"Commit thy way unto the LORD; trust also in him; and he shall bring it to pass." Psalms 37:5 (KJV)

"Commit thy works unto the LORD, and thy thoughts shall be established." Psalms 16:3 (KJV)

"Trust in the LORD with all thine heart; and lean not unto thine own understanding. In all thy ways acknowledge him, and he shall direct thy paths. Be not wise in thine own eyes: fear the LORD, and depart from evil. It shall be health to thy navel, and marrow to thy bones." Proverbs 3:5-8 (KJV)

WHEN PEOPLE ARE MEAN

It is difficult to be a part of today's society. It is evident that so many people have become angry, negative, quick-tempered, self-centered, and rude. It is a very large challenge to live a Godly life in the midst of a chaotic society. People you don't even know are mean to you. You can walk by someone, and smile and they will glare back, or look at you like you have a green monster sitting on your head. Many people, not all, test your patience and temperance daily.

It is important to remember you can live on Earth without becoming like society! A good goal is to not become like society and to not let society affect your relationship with God. Did someone make you mad? Take a breath and do not react in a negative way. No reaction is better than a negative one. Reacting in a way that matches their rudeness will make you just like the person who made you feel bad. Rise above it and walk on. One second of un-Godly behavior is not worth the lifetime of guilt. Take the high road. The high road leads to God. Their road is hazardous.

⬚ Temperance is the ability to maintain self-control in all aspects of life, but especially in behavior. **Temperance is another important puzzle piece to the true meaning of life.** Controlling moods, reactions and verbal tendencies is much more difficult than it sounds. It takes work, prayer, and strength. It is important to practice temperance to become less bound to react negatively so purity can be maintained.

"And to knowledge temperance; and to temperance patience; and to patience godliness;" 2 Peter 1:6 (KJV)

"Meekness, temperance: against such there is no law." Galatians 5:23 (KJV)

⬚ You cannot just have temperance. It takes work and in order to be able to master temperance, you need patience. Temperance and patience go hand in hand. How can you be able to practice self-control when you are not patient? Patience is defined as, "The suffering of afflictions, pain, toil, calamity, provocation or other evil, with a calm, unruffled temper; endurance without murmuring or fretfulness." (KJV Dictionary) Patience is needed to maintain temperance and keep cool while dealing with difficult people. We deal with difficult people every day, and this is why **patience is also an important puzzle piece to the true meaning of life.**

"And not only so, but we glory in tribulations also: knowing that tribulation worketh patience" Romans 5:3 (KJV)

"Giving no offence in any thing, that the ministry be not blamed: But in all things approving ourselves as the ministers of God, in much patience, in afflictions, in necessities, in distresses, In stripes, in imprisonments, in tumults, in labours, in watchings, in fastings; By pureness, by knowledge, by longsuffering, by kindness, by the Holy Ghost, by love unfeigned, By the word of truth, by the power of God, by the armour of righteousness on the right hand and on the left" 2 Corinthians 6:3-7 (KJV)

Revenge is not the way. It only leads us further from God. Don't become like society. Become like God instead. Although we are human and will never ever match the perfection of God, we want to live as much like God as possible so we can live an eternal life in his presence. Society is just a temporary background image to this earthly life. They are part of the big test. Keep your eye on the prize (eternal life), plan all your actions around pleasing God, and the rest won't even matter.

"See that none render evil for evil unto any man; but ever follow that which is good, both among yourselves, and to all men." 1 Thessalonians 5:15 (KJV)

"Thou shalt not avenge, nor bear any grudge against the children of thy people, but thou shalt love thy neighbour as thyself: I am the LORD." Leviticus 19:18 (KJV)

"Hatred stirreth up strifes: but love covereth all sins." Proverbs 10:12 (KJV)

"Say not thou, I will recompense evil; but wait on the LORD, and he shall save thee." Proverbs 20:22 (KJV)

"Ye have heard that it hath been said, An eye for an eye, and a tooth for a tooth: But I say unto you, That ye resist not evil: but whosoever shall smite thee on thy right cheek, turn to him the other also. And if any man will sue thee at the law, and take away thy coat, let him have thy cloke also And whosoever shall compel thee to go a mile, go with him twain. Give to him that asketh thee, and from him that would borrow of thee turn

not thou away. Ye have heard that it hath been said, Thou shalt love thy neighbour, and hate thine enemy.But I say unto you, Love your enemies, bless them that curse you, do good to them that hate you, and pray for them which despitefully use you, and persecute you; That ye may be the children of your Father which is in heaven: for he maketh his sun to rise on the evil and on the good, and sendeth rain on the just and on the unjust. " Matthew 5:38-45 (KJV)

NEEDS

Needs. This word seems to mean different things to different people—which is odd because needs should be the same for everyone. Your needs are God, food, water, shelter, clothing, knowledge, and sleep. Everyone needs these to survive. Everything else just falls under the want category. I know it is difficult to believe that your smart phone, daily frappe coffee, and that 10th pair of heels you've had your eye on are not needs--but it is true. Wanting something hard does not make it a need.

"But my God shall supply all your need according to his riches in glory by Christ Jesus." Philippians 4:19 (KJV)

"Be not ye therefore like unto them: for your Father knoweth what things ye have need of, before ye ask him." Matthew 6:8 (KJV)

"Neither was there any among them that lacked: for as many as were possessors of lands or houses sold them, and brought the prices of the things that were sold, and laid them down at the apostles' feet: and distribution was made unto every man according as he had need." Acts 4:34-35

"Let us therefore come boldly unto the throne of grace, that we may obtain mercy, and find grace to help in time of need." Hebrews 4:16 (KJV)

"For ye have need of patience, that, after ye have done the will of God, ye might receive the promise." Hebrews 10:36 (KJV)

🧩 In order to meet your needs, you must first seek the solution to meet your needs. If you are hungry, you need to find food. If you are thirsty, you will look for something to quench your thirst. If you are naked, you find clothes. **Seeking a solution is a definite puzzle piece in the true meaning of life.** Without the ability to seek, you will never find. Without the ability to find, you will never have the solutions to meet your needs. In order to keep fulfilling your needs, you must first seek God. God will meet all your needs if you invite him in your heart first. Seek God first and you will never be alone, and all your needs will be met.

"Seek ye the LORD, all ye meek of the earth, which have wrought his judgment; seek righteousness, seek meekness: it may be ye shall be hid in the day of the LORD'S anger." Zephania 2:3 (KJV)

"Seek the LORD, and his strength: seek his face evermore." Psalm 105:4 (KJV)

"But if from thence thou shalt seek the LORD thy God, thou shalt find him, if thou seek him with all thy heart and with all thy soul." Deuteronomy 4:29 (KJV)

"For here have we no continuing city, but we seek one to come." Hebrews 13:14 (KJV)

"Art thou bound unto a wife? seek not to be loosed. Art thou loosed from a wife? seek not a wife." 1 Corinthians 7:27 (KJV)

"And he did evil, because he prepared not his heart to seek the LORD." 2 Chronicles 12:14

"Salvation is far from the wicked: for they seek not thy statutes." Psalms 119:155 (KJV)

"Depart from evil, and do good; seek peace, and pursue it." Psalms 34:14 (KJV)

"Seek ye the LORD while he may be found, call ye upon him while he is near." Isaiah 55:6 (KJV)

"The young lions roar after their prey, and seek their meat from God." Psalms 104:21 (KJV)

"For all these things do the nations of the world seek after: and your Father knoweth that ye have need of these things." Luke 12:30 (KJV)

🧩 When you seek, you should find. Finding is the goal to seeking, and seeking is the action to complete the goal. **Both are important and both are puzzle pieces to the true meaning of life.** Why seek if you won't ever find? How can you find something specific if you don't actively seek? Find God first, and the rest will be shown to you, as long as you ask first. Sometimes you will find a gift from God when you weren't even seeking one. Surprise gifts from God are incredibly special. *"And the people, when they knew it, followed him: and he received them, and spake unto them of the kingdom of God, and healed them that had need of healing."* Luke 9:11 (KJV)

"Ask, and it shall be given you; seek, and ye shall find; knock, and it shall be opened unto you" Matthew 7:7

" So shalt thou find favour and good understanding in the sight of God and man." Proverbs 3:4 (KJV)

"They are all plain to him that understandeth, and right to them that find knowledge." Proverbs 8:9 (KJV)

"He that getteth wisdom loveth his own soul: he that keepeth understanding shall find good." Proverbs 19:8 (KJV)

"For the work of a man shall he render unto him, and cause every man to find according to his ways." Job 34:11 (KJV)

"And ye shall seek me, and find me, when ye shall search for me with all your heart." Jeremiah 29:13 (KJV)

"I love them that love me; and those that seek me early shall find me." Proverbs 8:17 (KJV)

"Because strait is the gate, and narrow is the way, which leadeth unto life, and few there be that find it." Matthew 7:14 (KJV)

"That they should seek the Lord, if haply they might feel after him, and find him, though he be not far from every one of us:" Acts 17:27 (KJV)

If you are praying for a lottery win, or a new car, or something that you want for vanity purposes, the reason you are not getting these things you pray for is because

God knows they are not a NEED, but a vain request for shallow purposes.

> *"Ye lust, and have not: ye kill, and desire to have, and cannot obtain: ye fight and war, yet ye have not, because ye ask not. Ye ask, and receive not, because ye ask amiss, that ye may consume it upon your lusts. "* James 4:2-3 (KJV)

IDOLATRY

So many people worship idols daily and don't even realize it. Did you know that raving over "celebrities" is idolizing? A celebrity is no more important than anyone else on this Earth. A person gets on a set and pretends they are someone else for a living. A person gets on a stage and belts out some songs for a living. (Usually they cannot even sing without the help of auto tune!) A person writes some books for a living. A person makes some YouTube videos for a living. Who cares. They, like you, are just people. There is no need to worship another human! They are just imperfect humans who sin and make bad choices, just like you. They are in the spotlight, only because another imperfect human put them there. Nobody on this planet is any better than anyone else on this planet.

"Set your affection on things above, not on things on the earth. For ye are dead, and your life is hid with Christ in God. When Christ, who is our life, shall appear, then shall ye also appear with him in glory. Mortify therefore your members which are upon the earth; fornication, uncleanness, inordinate affection, evil

concupiscence, and covetousness, which is idolatry"
Colossians 3:2-5 (KJV)

In the eyes of God, that celebrity is not ranked any higher than you—in fact, they may be ranked much lower due to the history of drugs, alcohol, sexual immorality, and long list of ended marriages. Never idolize. It is a waste of energy, time, and your soul.

"But the LORD said unto Samuel, Look not on his countenance, or on the height of his stature; because I have refused him: for the LORD seeth not as man seeth; for man looketh on the outward appearance, but the LORD looketh on the heart." 1 Samuel 16:7 (KJV)

"For by grace are ye saved through faith; and that not of yourselves: it is the gift of God: Not of works, lest any man should boast." Ephesians 2:8-9 (KJV)

*""Now the works of the flesh are manifest, which are these; Adultery, fornication, uncleanness, lasciviousness, **Idolatry**, witchcraft, hatred, variance, emulations, wrath, strife, seditions, heresies, Envyings, murders, drunkenness, revellings, and such like: of the which I tell you before, as I have also told you in*

time past, that they which do such things shall not inherit the kingdom of God. But the fruit of the Spirit is love, joy, peace, longsuffering, gentleness, goodness, faith, Meekness, temperance: against such there is no law." Galatians 5:19-23 (KJV)

"Put on the whole armour of God, that ye may be able to stand against the wiles of the devil. For we wrestle not against flesh and blood, but against principalities, against powers, against the rulers of the darkness of this world, against spiritual wickedness in high places." Ephesians 6:11-12 (KJV)

"Therefore seeing we have this ministry, as we have received mercy, we faint not; But have renounced the hidden things of dishonesty, not walking in craftiness, nor handling the word of God deceitfully; but by manifestation of the truth commending ourselves to every man's conscience in the sight of God. But if our gospel be hid, it is hid to them that are lost: In whom the god of this world hath blinded the minds of them which believe not, lest the light of the glorious gospel of Christ, who is the image of God, should shine unto them. 2 Corinthians 4:1-4 (KJV)

Why do so many people get so shocked when a celebrity dies? I'm sorry for the death of another human in any scenario, however, people die every single day, and they are not getting two-hour movies made on their life and remembrance videos posted on television. Watching this crap is a waste of time. You can be doing something much more helpful with your time than spending three hours researching a dead celebrity or watching videos on them. Take this time and go visit your own living loved ones. Take this time and go help others in the community—volunteer at a food pantry, go buy a homeless person a meal, go help a local school—even read the Bible--something other than idolizing a dead celebrity whom you didn't even know! I could assure you that if you died, a celebrity isn't going to even know or care. Why waste so much of your life on a person whom you never even met?

"Wherefore, my dearly beloved, flee from idolatry." 1 Corinthians 10:4 (KJV)

*"But the fearful, and unbelieving, and the abominable, and murderers, and whoremongers, and sorcerers, and **idolaters,** and all liars, shall have their part in the lake which burneth with fire and brimstone: which is the second death."* Revelation 21:8 (KJV)

Those celebrities that shocked people over their death usually have a history of sex, drugs, alcohol, and many other bad choices. I am not judging, just opening your eyes to the fact that being shocked over a death is probably not necessary. I'm shocked these people lived as long as they did—but not shocked when they die. Most people in the Hollywood spotlight sold their souls to the devil to get their "celebrity" status. Many women go to doctors to butcher their faces and bodies, so they look "acceptable" in Hollywood. The devil got into their mind and soul and told these people they weren't good enough. Instead of trusting God, they believed the devil and sold themselves out for false Earthly status.

Their bodies are God's temples, and he made their bodies and faces a certain way, not to be butchered or injected by an imperfect human to mold them into an unnatural form. Real is always better. If God wanted us to be Botox-injected, plastic molds, he would have made us this way. When someone gets plastic surgery, they are trying to improve God's work. Who are they to improve God? God doesn't need improvement and neither do his creations. Instead of trying to improve the external structure, these people need to try to improve their souls. Filling their souls with God has a much better result that injecting their face with Botox.

" Nay but, O man, who art thou that repliest against God? Shall the thing formed say to him that formed it, Why hast thou made me thus? Hath not the potter power over the clay, of the same lump to make one vessel unto honour, and another unto dishonour?" Romans 9:20-21 (KJV)

" Ye shall not make any cuttings in your flesh for the dead, nor print any marks upon you: I am the LORD." Leviticus 19:28 (KJV)

"Whose adorning let it not be that outward adorning of plaiting the hair, and of wearing of gold, or of putting on of apparel; But let it be the hidden man of the heart, in that which is not corruptible, even the

ornament of a meek and quiet spirit, which is in the sight of God of great price." 1 Peter 3:3-4 (KJV)

" What? know ye not that your body is the temple of the Holy Ghost which is in you, which ye have of God, and ye are not your own? For ye are bought with a price: therefore glorify God in your body, and in your spirit, which are God's." 1 Corinthians 6:19-20 (KJV)

"In like manner also, that women adorn themselves in modest apparel, with shamefacedness and sobriety; not with braided hair, or gold, or pearls, or costly array;" 1 Timothy 2:9 (KJV)

These people are not good examples for anyone. They are obviously not of God. *"He that is of God heareth God's words: ye therefore hear them not, because ye are not of God."* John 8:47 (KJV)   Putting them on a pedestal just because they are on a screen is actually pretty sinful. This is not how you get your puzzle pieces for the True Meaning of Life. Earthly celebrities are not part of the puzzle, so stop feeding the devil's circus acts and start feeding your soul to grow closer to God.

"Submit yourselves therefore to God. Resist the devil, and he will flee from you." James 4:7 (KJV)

"Having the understanding darkened, being alienated from the life of God through the ignorance that is in them, because of the blindness of their heart: Who being past feeling have given themselves over unto lasciviousness, to work all uncleanness with greediness. But ye have not so learned Christ;" Ephesians 4:18-20 (KJV)

"No man can serve two masters: for either he will hate the one, and love the other; or else he will hold to the one, and despise the other. Ye cannot serve God and mammon." Matthew 6:24 (KJV)

"Mammon" is defined as riches/wealth (KJV Dictionary)

Resist temptation to idolize anyone. Idolizing anything other than God is a broken commandment. No human on this earth is worth breaking a commandment or risking eternal life of your soul. If you get a tempting though to care about these false idols, think of God and his wishes for you and your soul and focus on how you can idolize God more and imperfect, sinful celebrities less.

A celebrity is a famous person, according to the Oxford Dictionary. Famous is defined as "widely known" according to Merriam Webster. The media makes people famous, not the talents of people. The media chooses who the spotlight shines on and the media is focusing on an evil agenda. The more people enforce the agenda, the more "famous" a "celebrity" becomes. This scenario is not of God. God created good and evil to give people a choice between good and evil. God does not tempt people with evil—people allow evil to tempt them. People who choose good are God's chosen people. People who choose evil belong to the devil. Most of Hollywood is like Hell on Earth—full of people who chose the evil way of the devil over God's Righteous path.

"I form the light, and create darkness: I make peace, and create evil: I the LORD do all these things." Isaiah 45:7 (KJV)

"A good man out of the good treasure of the heart bringeth forth good things: and an evil man out of the evil treasure bringeth forth evil things." Matthew 12:35 (KJV)

"Woe unto them that call evil good, and good evil; that put darkness for light, and light for darkness; that put bitter for sweet, and sweet for bitter!" Isaiah 5:20 (KJV)

" Let no man say when he is tempted, I am tempted of God: for God cannot be tempted with evil, neither tempteth he any man: But every man is tempted, when he is drawn away of his own lust, and enticed. Then when lust hath conceived, it bringeth forth sin: and sin, when it is finished, bringeth forth death." James 1:13:15 (KJV)

"Be not wise in thine own eyes: fear the LORD, and depart from evil." Proverbs 3:7 (KJV)

MOVING FORWARD

This may be a lot to take in. It's o.k. Please do not feel overwhelmed. Take it one day at a time and don't get too frustrated if you slip up. God knows you are a human and it is natural for you to sin. Overcoming sinful urges will get easier the more you do it, the more you pray, and the more you ask for forgiveness. As long as your heart wants to improve, you have the power of God helping you.

Don't take this book as a trend, and only follow it to "be trendy." Remember, living for society is not the answer, living for God is. Changing for the wrong reasons will cause an impure soul. You can't have a partly righteous life. It is all or nothing, so dive in whole-heartedly or don't dive in at all. You can fool other people, but you can't fool God.

As you can see, the true meaning of life isn't about anything you are probably focusing on. In the end, it doesn't matter what kind of car you had, how big your house was, how much money you made, what name brand clothing you wore, the job title or degrees you held, how many vacations you took, or the Earthly value of anything. What matters is the condition of your heart and soul. Did you complete the puzzle? Are you working hard each day to find those missing pieces?   Care less about shopping for material items and more about shopping for wisdom to be the best soul you can be. The goal is to impress God in the end, not humans in the process.

Guess what? Your earthly life is vain. Open your heart and soul and grow. Use your life on Earth to grow your soul—not your wallet. Put your true meaning of life puzzle together and in the end you will see the light—and in the process you will find happiness. *"Vanity of vanities, saith the Preacher, vanity of vanities; all is vanity."* Ecclesiastes 1:2 (KJV)

"Surely every man walketh in a vain shew: surely they are disquieted in vain: he heapeth up riches, and knoweth not who shall gather them." Psalm 39:6 (KJV)

"Favour is deceitful, and beauty is vain: but a woman that feareth the LORD, she shall be praised." Proverbs 31:30 (KJV)

"Turn away mine eyes from beholding vanity; and quicken thou me in thy way." Psalms 119:37 (KJV)

"The LORD knoweth the thoughts of man, that they are vanity." Psalms 94:11 (KJV)

"Wealth gotten by vanity shall be diminished: but he that gathereth by labour shall increase." Proverbs 13:11 (KJV)

"Therefore I hated life; because the work that is wrought under the sun is grievous unto me: for all is vanity and vexation of spirit." Ecclesiastes 2:17 (KJV)

"Therefore remove sorrow from thy heart, and put away evil from thy flesh: for childhood and youth are vanity." Ecclesiastes 11:10 (KJV)

"Let not him that is deceived trust in vanity: for vanity shall be his recompence." Job 15:31 (KJV)

"I have seen all the works that are done under the sun; and, behold, all is vanity and vexation of spirit." Ecclesiastes 1:14

"For all his days are sorrows, and his travail grief; yea, his heart taketh not rest in the night. This is also vanity." Ecclesiastes 2:23 (KJV)

It is better to continue sinning and not invite God into your heart than it is to invite him in, ask for forgiveness and continue the same evil acts day by day without any regard to God's wants.

"For if we sin wilfully after that we have received the knowledge of the truth, there remaineth no more sacrifice for sins, But a certain fearful looking for of judgment and fiery indignation, which shall devour the adversaries. " Hebrews 10:26-27 (KJV)

*"According as his divine power hath given unto us all things that pertain unto life and godliness, through the knowledge of him that hath called us to glory and virtue: Whereby are given unto us exceeding great and precious promises: that by these ye might be partakers of the divine nature, having escaped the corruption that is in the world through lust. And beside this, giving all diligence, add to your faith virtue; and to virtue knowledge; And to knowledge temperance; and to temperance patience; and to patience godliness; And to godliness brotherly kindness; and to brotherly kindness charity. For if these things be in you, and abound, they make you that ye shall neither be barren nor unfruitful in the knowledge of our Lord Jesus Christ. But he that lacketh these things is blind, and cannot see afar off, and hath forgotten that he was purged from his old sins. "*2 Peter:3-9 (KJV)

IN SUMMARY

PUZZLED?

Look at all the puzzle pieces. Now look at your life. Does your life contain all the puzzle pieces you need to live the True Meaning of Life? Do you have any missing pieces? Don't worry! Those missing pieces can be obtained by adding the missing actions to your life. Be honest with yourself. God knows what pieces are missing. We ALL have missing pieces. Some are more difficult to get. And some pieces may come easy for some but more difficult for others. The important thing is you try your best to get all the pieces and put them together while you still have time.

Do you have all the pieces?

⊞ Ten Commandments (you need to follow all 10 commandments to get this 1 piece!)

1. *Though shalt have no other god before Me.*

2. *Though shalt not make unto thee any graven image, or any likeness of any thing that is in heaven above or that is in the Earth beneath, or that is in the water under the Earth.*

3. *Thou shall not take the name of the Lord thy GOD in vain.*

4. *Remember the sabbath day, to keep it holy.*

5. *Honour thy father and thy mother: that thy days may be long upon the land which the LORD thy God giveth thee.*

6. *Thou shalt not kill.*

7. *Thou shalt not commit adultery.*

8. *Thou shalt not steal.*

9. *Thou shalt not bear false witness against thy neighbor.*

10. *Though shall not covet thy neighbour's house, thou shalt not covet they neighbor's wife, nor his manservant, nor his maidservant, nor his ox, nor his ass, nor anything that is thy neighbor's.*

⊞ Find and use God's Gift(s) (Any of these below or any not listed!)

- Wisdom (always seek this anyway!)
- Knowledge
- Faith
- The gifts of healing
- The working of miracles
- Prophecy
- Discerning of spirits
- Diverse kinds of tongues
- The interpretation of tongues

⊞ Believe in the Trinity

- Father (God)
- Son (Jesus)
- Holy Spirit (God in your heart)

⊞ Wisdom

- Study and you gain knowledge. Take the knowledge and combine it with truthful perspective and sound judgment and you have wisdom. Wisdom is taking the knowledge, filtering it through your heart and applying God's will to it to create a morally sound interpretation of the information gained.

⛶ Hard Work

- Work hard, rest in due time, work honestly and don't overcharge for your services. This is a form of robbery and deceit.
- Whether a person gets a paycheck or not, as long as they are performing important tasks, they are working….Rest is good, but there is a time for rest, and it shouldn't take the place of your daily work.

⛶ Diligence

- What is diligence? **<u>Diligence</u>:** Steady application in business of any kind; constant effort to accomplish what is undertaken; exertion of body or mind without unnecessary delay or sloth; due attention; industry; assiduity (KJV Dictionary). In any situation, not just in the workplace, diligence is necessary. It is the drive to force yourself past doubt, obstacles, and lack of faith. It is not the "I think I can," it is the "I know I can, I will, and I will not give up because God is with me." behind everything you do.

🧩 Righteousness

- Purity of heart and rectitude of life; conformity of heart and life to the divine law. (KJV Dictionary)
- Whether you are at home, at work, or at a store shopping, or making a social media video, God is observing your actions and thoughts.

🧩 Love

- *Love is patient, love is kind. It does not envy, it does not boast, it is not proud. It does not dishonor others, it is not self-seeking, it is not easily angered, it keeps no record of wrongs. Love does not delight in evil but rejoices with the truth. It always protects, always trusts, always hopes, always perseveres. Love never fails." 1 Corinthians 13:4-8 (NIV)*
- Without love, a marriage will fail—and a failed marriage will lead you to a bad place in God's eyes.

🧩 Being Honorable

- According to the KJV dictionary, honorable is defined as, "Possessing a high mind; actuated by principles of honor, or a scrupulous regard to probity, rectitude or reputation."
- Being an honorable person in all situations is important and leads to righteousness, good deeds, and honoring God.

🧩 Integrity

- "The entire, unimpaired state of any thing, particularly of the mind; moral soundness or purity; incorruptness; uprightness; honesty. integrity comprehends the whole moral character...." (Webster 1828)
- Also known as doing the right thing even when nobody is looking.

🧩 Abstain from sin.

- The refraining from an indulgence of appetite, or from customary gratifications of animal propensities. (Websters 1828)
- As a puzzle piece to the true meaning of life, abstinence is to refrain from any sinful act.

🧩 **Humble/Humility**

- **Humble**, according to the KJV dictionary is: "In an evangelical sense, having a low opinion of one's self, and a deep sense of unworthiness in the sight of God."

- **Humility** is: "freedom from pride and arrogance; humbleness of mind; a modest estimate of one's own worth; In theology, humility consists in lowliness of mind; a deep sense of one's own unworthiness in the sight of God, self-abasement, penitence for sin, and submission to the divine will." (KJV Dictionary)

- Live humble in all means and show humility to God.

🧩 **Discretion**

- Discretion needs to be used when making any decision in life, in order to stay on the road to righteousness and living for God.

- <u>**Discretion**</u>: "Prudence, or knowledge and prudence; that discernment which enables a person to judge critically of what is correct and proper, united with caution; nice discernment and judgment, directed by circumspection, and primarily regarding one's own conduct." (KJV Dictionary)

- It is absolutely necessary to use discretion when choosing your friends. Discretion needs to be used when making any decision in life, in order to stay on the road to righteousness and living for God.

⛉ Charity

- **<u>Charity</u>**: In a general sense, love, benevolence, good will; that disposition of heart which inclines men to think favorably of their fellow men to think favorably of their fellow men, and to do them good….Liberality to the poor, consisting in almsgiving or benefactions, or in gratuitous services to relieve them in distress. (KJV Dictionary)

- We are put here to help others overcome life and find God in the end. Charitable acts show others the miracle of God and give the recipient hope and faith in something more than the stresses they are facing on Earth. In order to provide charity, you must have brotherly kindness and love.

⛉ Brotherly Kindness

- Charity is an act of love and brotherly kindness. Brotherly kindness can be defined as a genuine concern for another. In order to give charity from the heart, you must have love and a genuine concern for the recipient(s) of your charitable act. Genuine concern for others is required to feel love and provide true charity. Without brotherly kindness, your acts are selfish, shallow, and void.

🧩 Purity

Purity: 1. Freedom from foreign admixture or heterogeneous matter; as the purity of water, of wine, of spirit; the purity of drugs; the purity of metals. 2. Cleanness; freedom from foulness or dirt; as the purity of a garment. 3. Freedom from guilt or the defilement of sin; innocence; as purity of heart or life. (KJV Dictionary)

- You cannot be pure if your image is not true. Think about it. You are mixing a pure image with secret sinful acts. If you buy an essential oil, you know if it says 100% pure, that it only contains 100% of the only stated on that bottle. Something can only be pure if it is not mixed with other things.

🧩 Faith

- Faith is defined by the KJV bible dictionary as, "The judgment that what another states or testifies is the truth." It can be difficult to believe in things beyond your visual capabilities. Without faith, you do not have God in your heart, or the belief in the Trinity.

🧩 Virtue

- Faith means nothing if you don't add virtue to it. Virtue is defined as strength and bravery (KJV Dictionary). If you don't have the bravery to show others or the strength to keep your faith, even in the toughest of times, then faith becomes temporary. Virtue must accompany faith.

🧩 Knowledge

- It is important that you know the difference between what is good and what is evil in the eyes of God. To do this, you need knowledge. Knowledge is defined as, " A clear and certain perception of that which exists, or of truth and fact" (KJV Dictionary). Knowledge will give you the ability to live the right way. Be careful, though. Once you have the knowledge to know better, you must do better.

⛶ Temperance

- Temperance is the ability to maintain self-control in all aspects of life, but especially in behavior. Controlling moods, reactions and verbal tendencies is much more difficult than it sounds. It takes work, prayer, and strength. It is important to practice temperance to become less bound to react negatively so purity can be maintained.

⛶ Patience

- Temperance and patience go hand in hand. How can you be able to practice self-control when you are not patient? Patience is defined as, "The suffering of afflictions, pain, toil, calamity, provocation or other evil, with a calm, unruffled temper; endurance without murmuring or fretfulness." (KJV Dictionary) Patience is needed to maintain temperance and keep cool while dealing with difficult people.

Godliness

- In order to abstain from sin, you must be able to portray Godliness. Godliness is, "A religious life; a careful observance of the laws of God and performance of religious duties, proceeding from love and reverence for the divine character and commands; Christian obedience."

Commit your life to God (Not Society)

- **Commit:** Literally, to send to or upon; to throw, put or lay upon. Hence, to give in trust; to put into the hands or power of another; to entrust; with to. (KJV Dictionary)

- Do everything with prayer and good intentions and the correct path will be shown to you by God. Commit yourself to God and he will get you through anything, including the evil words thrown your way when you turn your back on the sins of society.

Seek

- In order to meet your needs, you must first seek the solution to meet your needs. If you are hungry, you need to find food. If you are thirsty, you will look for something to quench your thirst. If you are naked, you find clothes. If you are lacking God in your heart, you need to seek him out. Without the ability to seek, you will never find. Without the ability to find, you will never have the solutions to meet your needs.

🧩 Find

- When you seek, you should find. Finding is the goal to seeking, and seeking is the action to complete the goal. Why seek if you won't ever find? How can you find if you don't actively seek? You won't always find the answer as you picture it in your mind. Sometimes the answer doesn't lie at the end of the seeking process. The answers you find can be disguised as a group of hidden treasures you discover during the seeking process. Remember, it isn't always what you think.

If you do not have the pieces, it's o.k. Take note of what each piece entails, make it a daily goal to follow all of the necessary steps. If you mess up, ask God for forgiveness and the strength to do better tomorrow. Work on your goals each day, and ask God each day to help and

you will gather all the pieces to the true meaning of life.
When you combine all the pieces together and build the
puzzle, the image is the light of God in your heart and an
eternal life with God.

*"Let us hear the conclusion of the whole
matter: Fear God, and keep his commandments: for this is
the whole duty of man. For God shall bring every work into
judgment, with every secret thing, whether it be good, or
whether it be evil."* Ecclesiastes 12:13-14 (KJV)

JESUS IS RETURNING

God created Jesus as a human form of his own perfection. Because the perfection of God was created in a human form, it allowed humans to understand the miracles that God can perform. God is larger than life, more perfect than anything and more than anything we can comprehend. Jesus died on the cross for our sins so we may believe in the power of God, be forgiven for our sins and have eternal life. Only those who believe in the trinity of God will have eternal life.

Jesus returned to God but promised he will return to Earth in the end times. Will you be ready? Can you face Jesus and feel good about the way you treated people, your life choices, and your priorities? If this concept seems scary, imagine the real situation. When you look at your life, what do you regret? Is it against God's will? Have you broken commandments or shamed God with your choices? Are you openly so proud that you see yourself as perfect? Whatever it is, there is time to ask for forgiveness and move forward in a more positive way. From this minute on, live for God. Gather your puzzle pieces and be ready for that big day when HE returns.

Use each day as a fresh start and create a new path that leads away from your past sin and guides you closer to God and an eternal life. It is never too late to become the person God meant you to be. This does not mean making everyone accept your overly-proud demeanor because you are you—this means asking God to help you change the things that are not acceptable to him and forgive your sins. This also means you need to make a choice to live for him and not your own selfish wants. Once you do this, commit to it, pray for help, see your flaws, and become humble in your imperfections, you will be on your way to eternal life.

BE READY because NOBODY KNOWS when HE will Return, we just know HE WILL.

"In a moment, in the twinkling of an eye, at the last trump: for the trumpet shall sound, and the dead shall be raised incorruptible, and we shall be changed." 1 Corinthians 15:52 (KJV)

" For the Lord himself shall descend from heaven with a shout, with the voice of the archangel, and with the trump of God: and the dead in Christ shall rise first: Then we which are alive and remain shall be caught up together with them in the clouds, to meet the Lord in the air: and so shall we ever be with the Lord." 1 Thessalonians 4:16-17 (KJV)

"Jesus said unto her, I am the resurrection, and the life: he that believeth in me, though he were dead, yet shall he live" John 11:25 (KJV)

"So Christ was once offered to bear the sins of many; and unto them that look for him shall he appear the second time without sin unto salvation" Hebrews 9:28 (KJV)

"And there shall be signs in the sun, and in the moon, and in the stars; and upon the earth distress of nations, with perplexity; the sea and the waves roaring; Men's hearts failing them for fear, and for looking after those things which are coming on the earth: for the powers of heaven shall be shaken. And then shall they see the Son

of man coming in a cloud with power and great glory. And when these things begin to come to pass, then look up, and lift up your heads; for your redemption draweth nigh." Luke 21:25-28 (KJV)

"Behold, he cometh with clouds; and every eye shall see him, and they also which pierced him: and all kindreds of the earth shall wail because of him. Even so, Amen." Revelation 1:7 (KJV)

"And I give unto them eternal life; and they shall never perish, neither shall any man pluck them out of my hand. My Father, which gave them me, is greater than all; and no man is able to pluck them out of my Father's hand. I and my Father are one." John 10:28-30 (KJV)

"Watch therefore, for ye know neither the day nor the hour wherein the Son of man cometh." Matthew 25:13 (KJV)

"For as the lightning cometh out of the east, and shineth even unto the west; so shall also the coming of the Son of man be." Matthew 24:27 (KJV)

"So Christ was once offered to bear the sins of many; and unto them that look for him shall he appear the second time without sin unto salvation." Hebrews 9:28 (KJV)

"But of that day and hour knoweth no man, no, not the angels of heaven, but my Father only." Matthew 24:36 (KJV)

"Watch therefore, for ye know neither the day nor the hour wherein the Son of man cometh." Matthew 25:13 (KJV)

"For the Son of man shall come in the glory of his Father with his angels; and then he shall reward every man according to his works." Matthew 16:27 (KJV)

"And as he sat upon the mount of Olives, the disciples came unto him privately, saying, Tell us, when shall these things be? and what shall be the sign of thy coming, and of the end of the world? And Jesus answered and said unto them, Take heed that no man deceive you. For many shall come in my name, saying, I am Christ; and shall deceive many. And ye shall hear of wars and rumours of wars: see that ye be not troubled: for all these things must come to pass, but the end is not yet. For nation shall rise against nation, and kingdom against kingdom: and there shall be famines, and pestilences, and earthquakes, in divers places. All these are the beginning of sorrows. Then shall they deliver you up to be afflicted, and shall kill you: and ye shall be hated of all nations for my name's sake. And then shall many be offended, and shall betray one another, and shall hate one another. And many false prophets shall rise, and shall deceive many. And because iniquity shall abound, the love of many shall wax cold. But

he that shall endure unto the end, the same shall be saved. And this gospel of the kingdom shall be preached in all the world for a witness unto all nations; and then shall the end come. When ye therefore shall see the abomination of desolation, spoken of by Daniel the prophet, stand in the holy place, (whoso readeth, let him understand:) Then let them which be in Judaea flee into the mountains: Let him which is on the housetop not come down to take any thing out of his house: Neither let him which is in the field return back to take his clothes. And woe unto them that are with child, and to them that give suck in those days! But pray ye that your flight be not in the winter, neither on the sabbath day: For then shall be great tribulation, such as was not since the beginning of the world to this time, no, nor ever shall be. And except those days should be shortened, there should no flesh be saved: but for the elect's sake those days shall be shortened. Then if any man shall say unto you, Lo, here is Christ, or there; believe it not. For there shall arise false Christs, and false prophets, and shall shew great signs and wonders; insomuch that, if it were possible, they shall deceive the very elect. Behold, I have told you before. Wherefore if they shall say unto you, Behold, he is in the desert; go not forth: behold, he is in the secret chambers;

believe it not. For as the lightning cometh out of the east, and shineth even unto the west; so shall also the coming of the Son of man be. For wheresoever the carcase is, there will the eagles be gathered together. Immediately after the tribulation of those days shall the sun be darkened, and the moon shall not give her light, and the stars shall fall from heaven, and the powers of the heavens shall be shaken: And then shall appear the sign of the Son of man in heaven: and then shall all the tribes of the earth mourn, and they shall see the Son of man coming in the clouds of heaven with power and great glory. And he shall send his angels with a great sound of a trumpet, and they shall gather together his elect from the four winds, from one end of heaven to the other. Now learn a parable of the fig tree; When his branch is yet tender, and putteth forth leaves, ye know that summer is nigh: So likewise ye, when ye shall see all these things, know that it is near, even at the doors. Verily I say unto you, This generation shall not pass, till all these things be fulfilled. Heaven and earth shall pass away, but my words shall not pass away. But of that day and hour knoweth no man, no, not the angels of heaven, but my Father only. But as the days of Noe were, so shall also the coming of the Son of man be. For as in the days that were before the flood they were eating and drinking, marrying and giving in marriage, until the day that Noah entered into the ark, And knew not until the flood came, and took them all away; so shall also the coming of the Son of man be. Then shall two be in the field; the one shall be taken, and the other left. Two women shall be grinding at the mill; the one shall be taken, and the other left. Watch therefore: for ye know not what hour your Lord doth come. But know this, that if the goodman of the house had known in what watch the thief would come, he would have watched, and would not have suffered his house to be broken up. Therefore be ye also ready: for in such an hour as ye think not the Son of man cometh. Who then is a faithful and wise servant, whom his lord hath made ruler over his household, to give them meat in due season? Blessed is that servant, whom his lord when he cometh shall find so doing. Verily I say unto you, That he shall make him ruler over all his goods. But and if that evil servant shall say in his heart, My lord delayeth his coming; And shall begin to smite his fellow servants, and to eat and drink with the drunken; The lord of that servant shall come in a day when he looketh not for him, and in an hour that he is not aware of, And shall cut him asunder, and appoint him his portion with the hypocrites: there shall be weeping and gnashing of teeth." Matthew 24:3-51

150

<h1 style="text-align:center">GLOSSARY</h1>

<u>Acquaintance</u>: Familiar knowledge; a state of being acquainted, or of having intimate or more than slight or superficial knowledge; (KJV Dictionary)

<u>Alms</u>: Any thing given gratuitously to relieve the poor, such as money, food, or clothing, otherwise called charity. (KJV Dictionary)

<u>Benefaction</u>: Donation or gift (Merriam-Webster)

<u>Charity</u>: In a general sense, love, benevolence, good will; that disposition of heart which inclines men to think favorably of their fellow men to think favorably of their fellow men, and to do them good….Liberality to the poor, consisting in almsgiving or benefactions, or in gratuitous services to relieve them in distress. (KJV Dictionary)

<u>Covet</u>: To desire inordinately; to desire that which it is unlawful to obtain or possess; in a bad sense. (KJV Dictionary)

<u>Diligence</u>: Steady application in business of any kind; constant effort to accomplish what is undertaken; exertion of body or mind without unnecessary delay or sloth; due attention; industry; assiduity.

<u>Discretion</u>: Prudence, or knowledge and prudence; that discernment which enables a person to judge critically of what is correct and proper, united with caution; nice discernment and judgment, directed by circumspection, and primarily regarding one's own conduct. (KJV Dictionary)

<u>Effeminate</u>: Having the qualities of the female sex; soft or delicate to an unmanly degree; tender; womanish; voluptuous. (KJV Dictionary)

<u>Enemy</u>: A foe; an adversary. A private enemy is one who hates another and wishes him injury, or attempts to do him injury to gratify his own malice or ill will. (KJV Dictionary

<u>Exploiter</u>: 1. In a ludicrous sense, a great act of wickedness. (KJV Dictionary) 2. to make use of meanly or unfairly for one's own advantage (Merriam-Webster

<u>Faith</u>: The judgment that what another states or testifies is the truth. (KJV Dictionary)

<u>Frenemy</u>: A person who is or pretends to be a friend but who is also in some ways an enemy or rival (Merriam-Webster)

<u>Friend</u>: One who is attached to another by affection; one who entertains for another sentiments of esteem, respect, and affection, which lead him to desire his company, and to seek to promote his happiness and prosperity; opposed to foe or enemy. (KJV Dictionary)

Godliness: A religious life; a careful observance of the laws of God and performance of religious duties, proceeding from love and reverence for the divine character and commands; Christian obedience. (KJV Dictionary)

Honorable: Possessing a high mind; actuated by principles of honor, or a scrupulous regard to probity, rectitude, or reputation. (Websters 1828 Dictionary)

Humble: In an evangelical sense, having a low opinion of one's self, and a deep sense of unworthiness in the sight of God. (KJV Dictionary)

Humility: freedom from pride and arrogance; humbleness of mind; a modest estimate of one's own worth; In theology, humility consists in lowliness of mind; a deep sense of one's own unworthiness in the sight of God, self-abasement, penitence for sin, and submission to the divine will." (KJV Dictionary)

ICHTHUS: It is said that the name ICHTHUS is an acrostic word formed to filter non-believers from believers in various situations. The easy-to-draw image was shown as a secret code to affirm their belief in God to other believers. Because Jewish people were against Christian beliefs, Christians used a secret code only they knew to represent their dedication to God. **I**esous (Jesus) **Ch**ristos (Christ) **Th**eous (God) **U**IOS (Son) **S**oter (Savior) (Also called the Jesus Fish)

Integrity: The entire, unimpaired state of any thing, particularly of the mind; moral soundness or purity; incorruptness; uprightness; honesty. integrity comprehends the whole moral character…." (Webster 1828) ****Also known as doing the right thing even when nobody is looking.***

Iniquity: Injustice; unrighteousness; a deviation from rectitude; a sin or crime; wickedness; any act of injustice. (KJV Dictionary)

Knowledge: A clear and certain perception of that which exists, or of truth and fact

LGBTQ: Lesbian, Gay, Bisexual, Transexual, Queer—All abominations in God's eyes.

Thou shalt not lie with mankind, as with womankind: it is abomination Leviticus 18:22

Nevertheless, to avoid fornication, let every man have his own wife, and let every woman have her own husband. 1 Corinthians 7:2

Mammon: Riches/wealth (KJV Dictionary)

Marriage: The act of uniting a man and woman for life; wedlock; the legal union of a man and woman for life. (KJV Dictionary)

Neighbor: is referred to not the person living next door to you, but as a person out in the community. A fellow child of God. A person who helps others. Do unto others as you want others to do unto you. Anyone who lives this way is a neighbor. So be a neighbor to others.

Patience: The suffering of afflictions, pain, toil, calamity, provocation, or other evil, with a calm, unruffled temper; endurance without murmuring or fretfulness." (KJV Dictionary)

Pride: an unreasonable conceit of one's own superiority in talents, beauty, wealth, accomplishments, rank, or elevation in office, which manifests itself in lofty airs, distance, reserve, and often in contempt of others." (KJV Dictionary)

Purity: 1. Freedom from foreign admixture or heterogeneous matter; as the purity of water, of wine, of spirit; the purity of drugs; the purity of metals. 2. Cleanness; freedom from foulness or dirt; as the purity of a garment. 3. Freedom from guilt or the defilement of sin; innocence; as purity of heart or life. (KJV Dictionary)

Righteousness: Purity of heart and rectitude of life; conformity of heart and life to the divine law. (KJV Dictionary)

Temperance: is the ability to maintain self-control in all aspects of life, but especially in behavior.

Traitor: One who betrays His trust. (KJV Dictionary)

Vain: 1. too proud of your own appearance, abilities, achievements, etc. 2. having no success: not producing a desired result (Merriam Webster)

Virtue: strength and bravery (KJV Dictionary)

Wisdom: Properly, having knowledge; hence, having the power of discerning and judging correctly, or of discriminating between what is true and what is false; between what is fit and proper, and what is improper (Webster 1828)

⚲ **Christian Fish (ICHTHUS):**

Do you wonder what the meaning behind the symbols above are? It is said that the name ICHTHUS is an acrostic word formed to filter non-believers from believers in various situations. The easy-to-draw image was shown as a secret code to affirm their belief in God to other believers. Because Jewish people were against Christian beliefs, Christians used a secret code only they knew to represent their dedication to God.

Iesous (Jesus)
Christos (Christ)
Theous (God)
UIOS (Son)
Soter (Savior)

Mustard Plant. A mustard plant is a representation of how our faith can start as tiny as a mustard seed, yet grow strong with firm roots, like a mustard plant.

"Which indeed is the least of all seeds: but when it is grown, it is the greatest among herbs, and becometh a tree, so that the birds of the air come and lodge in the branches thereof." Matthew 13:32 (KJV)

"And Jesus said unto them, Because of your unbelief: for verily I say unto you, If ye have faith as a grain of mustard seed, ye shall say unto this mountain, Remove hence to yonder place; and it shall remove; and

nothing shall be impossible unto you." Matthew 17:20 (KJV)

✝ **Cross:** The cross that Jesus bared was crucifixion. Jesus' crucifixion was a violent act where Jesus was actually nailed to a cross. The cross is still a symbol that represents the pain and suffering Jesus went through so or sins could be forgiven, and we can have eternal life.
For imperfect humans to "take up the cross," this means, according to KJV dictionary, "to submit to troubles and afflictions from love to Christ."   In order for a person to repent from sins and be forgiven, they must first suffer consequences of those sins and show humility to God. This is a form of carrying a cross.

"And he that taketh not his cross, and followeth after me, is not worthy of me." Matthew 10:38 (KJV)

"And whosoever doth not bear his cross, and come after me, cannot be my disciple." Luke 14:27 (KJV)

All of these symbols are important icons of faith, suffering and believing in the power of God to pull us through any situation in our Earthly lives so our soul can have eternal life.

INDEX